Underwater Video For Scuba Divers

An Easy To Understand Guide to Digital Underwater Video from GoPro to Professional Filmmaking

Jill Heinerth
Professional Filmmaker & Video Columnist for DIVER Magazine

www.IntoThePlanet.com

Published by:

Heinerth Productions Inc.

5989 NE County Road 340

High Springs, Florida 32643 USA

First published 2016

All photography and text by Jill Heinerth

This manual is not intended to be used as a substitute for proper dive training. Diving is a dangerous sport and training should only be conducted under the safe supervision of an active diving instructor until you are fully qualified, and then, only in conditions and circumstances which are as good or better than the conditions in which you were trained. Careful risk assessment, continuing education and skill practice may lessen your likelihood of an accident, but are never a guarantee for complete safety.

This book assumes a basic knowledge of diving technique and should be used to complement a training course specializing in underwater photography techniques.

www.IntoThePlanet.com

ISBN 978-1-940944-21-0

About the Author - Jill Heinerth

"More people have been to the moon than to places that Jill Heinerth has explored deep inside our watery planet. A world class technical diver and filmmaker, Jill's extraordinary path from under Antarctic icebergs to tropical blue holes is proof that real life is far more exciting than fiction."

- James Cameron, Director

In recognition of her lifetime achievement, Jill was awarded the first Sir Christopher Ondaatje Medal for Exploration. Established by the Royal Canadian Geographical Society in 2013, the medal recognizes singular achievements and the pursuit of excellence by an outstanding Canadian explorer.

Jill is a Fellow of the Explorer's Club and an inductee in the inaugural class of the Women Diver's Hall of Fame. She received the Wyland ICON Award, an honor she shares with several of her underwater heroes including Jacques Cousteau, Robert Ballard and Dr. Sylvia Earle. She was named a *"Living Legend"* by Sport Diver Magazine and selected as Scuba Diving Magazine's *"Sea Hero of the Year 2012."*

With her educational mission, the *"We Are Water Project,"* she has produced a documentary film, a live presentation and interactive web resources to help steer an educational effort for everyday behavioral changes that will lead to greater access to and preservation of our endangered fresh water resources. In support of this effort, Jill and husband Robert McClellan rode their bicycles 4,300 miles, unsupported, across Canada, from British Columbia to Newfoundland in 2013, meeting people and through presentations to groups large and small, spreading the message of "Water Literacy."

Jill is the video columnist for DIVER Magazine and writes regularly for publications including Scuba Diving, Sport Diver and others.

Jill's website *IntoThePlanet.com* showcases her photography and international speaking engagements, and her interactive blogs. Born in Canada, Jill lives with her husband Robert, in North Florida, where she starts most days with a refreshing swim in the clear water of her local spring.

Scope of This Book

Underwater Video for Scuba Divers covers the fundamentals for underwater videography. It provides basic instructions for using simple, inexpensive underwater cameras and serves as a foundation for divers who are interested in pursuing advanced shooting with more complex systems. The book is filled with anecdotes from my personal journey through the world of filmmaking and photography. Filled with expedition tales and first person accounts, I hope you'll find this guide to be your virtual mentor.

The Basics

Motivation

Whether you are a new diver or an experienced professional, it is appealing to capture the memories of your diving adventures. *Underwater Video for Scuba Divers* serves as an introduction to getting the most out of your underwater filming opportunities. Whether you are snorkeling in the crystal clear shallows of a freshwater lake, or diving on deep ocean walls, this guide will help you understand the capabilities of your camera system and improve your ability to bring back quality videos to share with your family, friends and dive buddies.

Underwater videography combines creativity with adventure and offers a diver boundless prospects for recording subjects that few people have ever seen. Underwater videography enhances travel opportunities, adds fun and exciting challenges to your diving excursions and gives you an interesting new pastime to share with your buddy. However, adding a task-load to your recreational diving activities requires that you sharpen your buoyancy and general diving skills to protect yourself and the environment. This guidebook will assist you in improving your awareness and technical diving skills as well as your general knowledge of videography and composition for both topside and underwater filming activities.

Safety First

Swimming with a Camera

Swimming with a camera system can be very challenging. Small compact cameras such as GoPros can be easily stashed in a BCD pocket, but larger cameras will create drag as well as a change in body trim. A large camera system with attached video lights will reduce swim speed and range and will usually occupy both hands. It is advisable to trim your video equipment to as close to neutral as possible. Excessively buoyant systems can be as troublesome as negatively buoyant packages. Very small trim weights (like stainless steel washers) can be affixed to a housing to trim the position and adjust buoyancy. Hollow, sealed camera arms may be utilized to increase positive buoyancy of heavy lights and a special incompressible material called syntactic foam can be added to a package that is unreasonably heavy. Some divers make their own custom, sealed PVC tubes to lighten their load. Flexible air cells are not suitable, because they require continual adjustment as depth varies. The buoyancy characteristics of housings and lights are often noted in their technical specifications and should be reviewed before purchase.

Beyond the buoyancy of the package itself, a camera system may alter your personal trim in the water. Holding a slightly negative housing in front of your body will tip your center of gravity to a more head-down position. A positively buoyant housing will pull your upper body higher and, in the case of cave or wreck dives, may cause you to create more silt with your fins. Prior to taking a single frame of video, it is recommended that divers assemble their camera package and swim with it for a dive or two. Determining how it may affect trim and speed, before adding filmmaking goals, is time well spent. Your dive buddy can assist you with constructive comments about your streamlining and trim.

Underwater videography is a task-loaded activity that will add significant challenges to your diving. Whether you are the model or the shooter, you will learn to refine your buoyancy to a high level of proficiency. You will also find video dives to be more physically and mentally tiring than most. As a creative endeavor, videography uses the part of your brain that is not very good at keeping track of time and numbers. You will need to remain vigilant about watching your air supply and depth. Some shooters set their dive watch to beep every five minutes to remind them to check their consumables. Dive buddies and models should be advised to be more active observers of a task-loaded videographer.

Some divers choose to attach their camera systems to their body to prevent accidental loss. However, lanyards and other clips can create an unnecessary danger. If there is a need to drop a weight belt, it can become entangled in a lanyard system. For this reason alone, you should always be prepared and able to ditch your camera system in an emergency. It may be an expensive loss, but surely not worth your life. If you are unwilling to drop your camera for the sake of your life, then you may want to reconsider your motivations for pursuing underwater videography.

The author filming for the BBC in North Florida. Photo: Anthony Lenzo

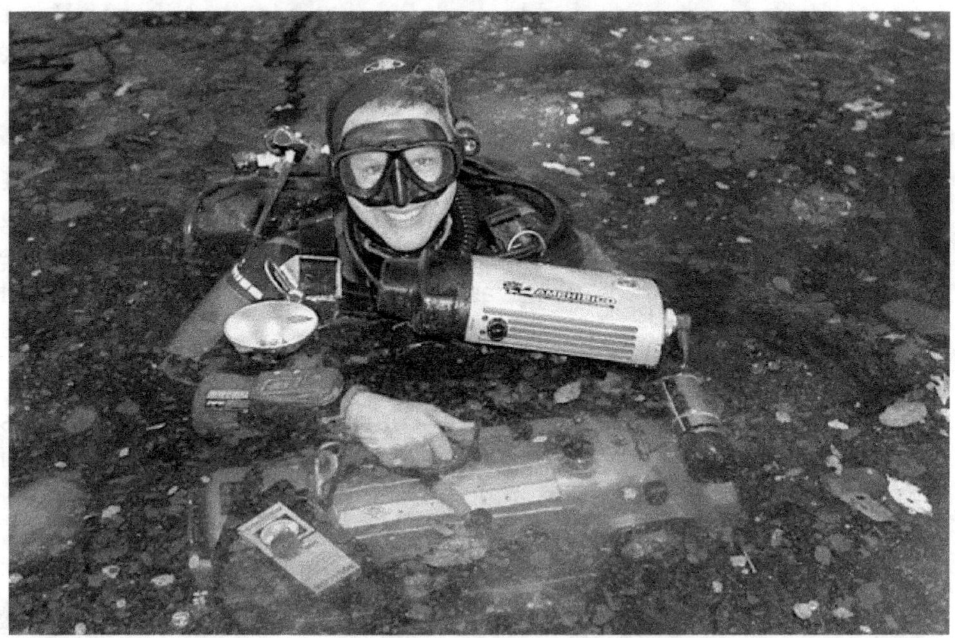

A Flood of Troubles

In the early nineties, I made some serious life changes. Disenchanted by my business partners, I decided to sell my portion of a Toronto advertising business and head to the Cayman Islands. I loved the creative aspects of my career, but needed to find a way to weave that with my love for diving. I landed at a small resort on the secluded East End of Grand Cayman. At the twelve-room resort, I would be responsible for diving, marketing and anything from cooking meals to painting walls. It was a time of great freedom. I sold my business, left my boyfriend, had a yard sale and moved south with little more than a suitcase of bikinis and shorts. Knowing that my business partners would be slowly paying me back on a twenty-year note, gave me the comfort of having a nest egg to return to when needed.

On a sunny day close to Christmas, I got a disturbing phone call. A colleague in Toronto gave me the bad news that my former partners had literally closed the business one night and re-opened the following morning under a new name, using all the equipment for chattel on loans. They had decided to evade their debt to me and move on without financial constraint. My nest egg was gone. Thankfully, it was my day off, and I decided that the best way to process the news was to go do what I loved most. I headed out on the morning dive boat and dropped down the wall with my camera. At 165 feet, I felt a tremendous concussion and looked down to see my Nikonos V with 15 mm lens rapidly spewing bubbles. With a decompression obligation hanging over my head, there was nothing to do but watch the salty water seep into the camera body. The system was destroyed.

But at times like these, we often get the greatest clarity. Did I want to return to Toronto and begin a multi-year litigation of revenge against my former partners? With nothing more than a few clothes and a stray dog named Spot, was this the direction I wanted my life to take?

But whether it is a real stripping down to the basics or a metaphoric one, this is how we choose our best course in life. With nothing else to distract me from my goals, I knew that I wanted to be an underwater photographer and filmmaker, no matter the cost.

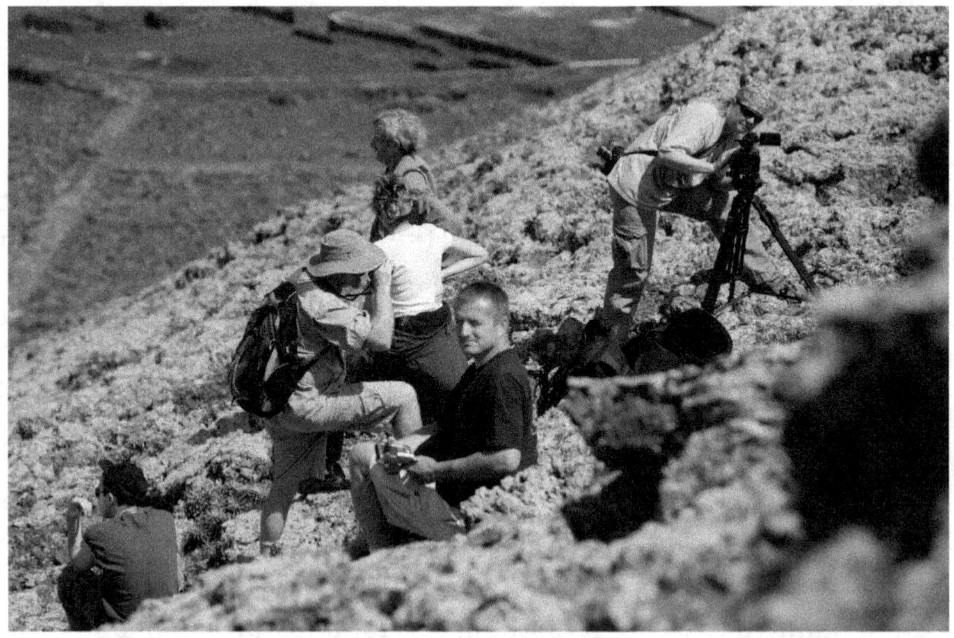

The author shooting expedition coverage on the peak of the Monte Corona volcano in Lanzarote. Photo: Jim Rozzi

Assembling a Crew

How to Make Shooting Underwater Video a Team Sport

To give an underwater scene a sense of scale, it is usually best to use a dive buddy as a model. Viewers who have not experienced a reef, wreck or cave, have no idea how vast the environment is unless you give them something familiar with which to interpret scale. Your model can double as your safety diver, with skills to protect the environment and execute a safe and successful shoot.

When models are used for complex lighting scenarios, they will be holding and directing lights for you. For best results, it is important that they understand the creative vision and composition you have in mind for a shot. Simple hands signals for lighting, action and posing are important to communicate before leaving the surface. An underwater notebook or slate will also be beneficial for communication regarding complex shots. If you can afford it, a full-face mask (FFM) with earpieces such as the *Buddy Phone* system will help you send vocal commands to your team.

Buddy Planning

Prior to the dive, ensure that your buddy is completely aware of their role as model or safety diver or both. If you make the dive buddy an active part of the shoot, they will stay engaged in the process and contribute to a safer environment. Review signals and refresh your buddy about any shots you would like to set up. Coach them on body position and trim. Remind them to be vigilant in helping you keep track of gas supplies and dive plans. Advise them to notify you if your position might cause damage to the environment.

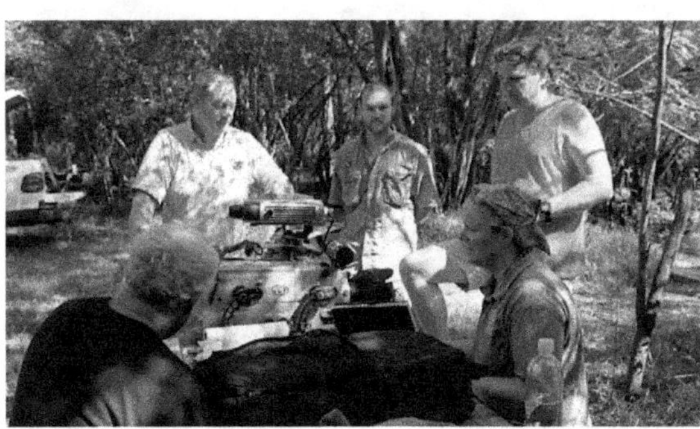

Team planning and rehearsal is critical when underwater time is limited by exposure, decompression and gas supply.

Environmental Factors

Temperature

There are several aspects of temperature that may influence your diving and ability to shoot. Low surface and water temperatures may present physical challenges, and might also have an impact on your camera and batteries.

Preparing to Shoot Your Best Video in Cold Water

You've dedicated years of training and invested plenty of money on equipment to be ready to visit the wreck of the Forest City in Tobermory or the Rose Castle in Bell Island, Newfoundland. You are sweating profusely on the dock as you ease into your heavy drysuit and thick undergarments, preparing to jump into the Zodiac for a very special dive. It might be creeping over 30°C topside, but you know you have to be prepared for the chilling plunge to 4°C on the bottom. It's worth it. Now is the moment you can shoot a video to bring home to your friends and family. But, as important as it is to be personally prepared for the cold, you also need to take special precautions for your camera.

Taking a warm camera into freezing waters can result in some unpleasant surprises. Whether you are shooting a GoPro or a professional video camera in a specialized underwater housing, you may experience the much dreaded lens fog. You excitedly compose your subject through the viewfinder, and it starts to glaze over with a white film of moisture. You clear your mask, rub down the viewfinder and finally rotate the dome around so you can peer into the lens. Fog! Again! Plunging deeper through the thermocline the fog gradually takes over the housing, ruining any attempts at getting a clear shot. You might as well look around and enjoy the scenery instead of shooting.

There are a few simple tips that can help prevent fog from forming inside your housing:

1. Prepare and load your camera in a dry and stable atmospheric and temperature conditions, similar to that of your dive if possible. Don't take a camera from air conditioning to the outside and load it into a housing on a hot day. It will fog the lens and viewfinder. On a recent trip to the Arctic, I loaded and unloaded my camera on deck

in the shade. The camera and housing stayed cool and protected inside a Nanuk hard case while underway.

2. Try using desiccant inside the housing to absorb moisture. The desiccant can take the form of small paper strips that are pressed into the corners of GoPro housings, or it may be the familiar pouches filled with silica beads. The pouches can be carefully attached with Velcro or gaffer tape inside larger housings.

3. Use dry scuba tank air to prepare the housing. Use a spray nozzle to blow dry air into the housing prior to loading. Some professionals even go to the extremes of using nitrogen to purge the housing, but this is likely more than you will need to do!

4. Be prepared to take care of your camera in between dives. It needs to stay out of the direct sun where it can get overheated, ruining your second dive. Travel with a collapsible cooler that can be filled with water or ice or use your Nanuk or Pelican case as sun protection for the housing. Rinse tanks can be a safe refuge as long as your housing is not banging around with other cameras in a way that could damage the dome port.

5. In the event that there is no way to dunk your camera in a cooler or tank, then at least wrap it in a wet towel and douse it with cold water once in a while. Keep it out of the sun and try to keep the temperature as cool as possible.

6. If a boat is stationary, then carefully hang your camera into the water on a gear line off the back of the boat. Don't forget it if the captain starts the engine!

7. Use a vacuum pump to seal your housing. It not only checks the security of your seal but also tends to reduce fogging issues.

Beyond your camera, you may need to think about preparation for yourself in cold temperatures. Camera operators are usually the first off the boat and the last to finish a dive. You need to stay warm and be able to operate your controls in heavy gloves and cold temperatures. For many years I used three-finger wet neoprene lobster gloves, but they are sometimes too thick to effectively operate all the controls on my cameras today. Now I use dry gloves mounted on rings on my dry suit. My preference is Kubi rings with Santi heated under gloves. If I know I will be subjected to long, cold submersions, I utilize my Santi heated gloves with a heated vest or full heated suit. With a hip mounted battery pack, I can run a heated undergarment and gloves for two hours. If I use the heater judiciously it lasts even longer. I've managed up to five hours in near freezing water and remained relatively comfortable. For me, the kicker is always my hands. They are tightly gripping the housing handles and operating controls. They get really cold without the additional heat.

If you are considering going the cheap route and using disposable chemical heat packs, think again. They may be okay in shallow water, but as the depth increases, so will the partial pressure of oxygen. By the time you reach 130 feet deep, they will burning fast and hot as if they were placed in an equivalent 100% oxygen environment. My colleague once taped these packs to his toes to ward off the cold. The three-hour dive resulted in serious second-degree burns and significant blistering, although he did say that it felt good at the time!

Chemical heat packs have one good use though. They can help keep hands and batteries warm in extreme topside conditions. If you choose the rechargeable type of packs made of gel that activates with a small metal disk, then they can be placed in a cooler to keep the camera from freezing hard in really rough conditions on top of the ice. Submerging your camera in a large bucket of water will generally keep it ice free between dives in all but the most extreme conditions.

Cold water diving is extremely rewarding. You'll likely get to see things underwater that few people have witnessed. You'll return home with breathtaking images, enthralling your audience with unique and extremely tough to acquire video footage.

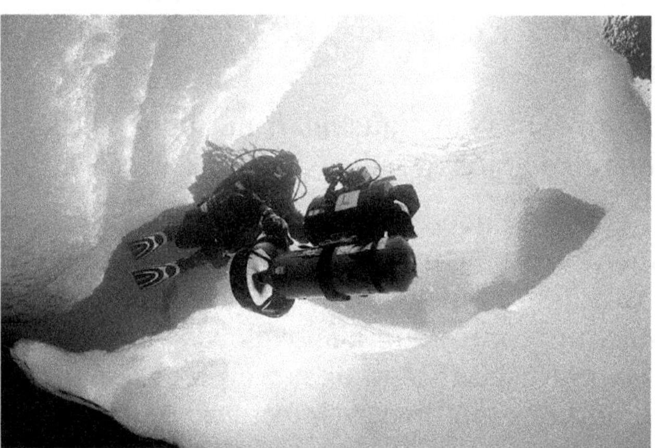

Becky Kagan Schott working in the Arctic with the Sedna EPIC Expedition. Photo by Jill Heinerth courtesy of SednaEpic.com

Visibility

Good visibility will significantly increase your chances of getting great shots, but poor conditions still offer many opportunities. When the water is murky, macro shooting is a good choice, since the camera will be placed very close to the subject. Similarly, a wide-angle lens allows the diver to get closer to the subject and thus reduce the amount of filtering water between the subject and the lens.

Some water conditions contain a great deal of tiny, solid particles, known as particulate, and the video light reflected from these specks into the lens, creates an undesirable situation known as "backscatter." Lights mounted on arms allow the shooter to angle the light towards the subject to reduce backscattering. Shooting in shallow water with bright natural light may permit you to use a filter instead of a light, thus completely preventing backscatter. You might be surprised at what your camera can see in ambient light scenarios. The footage might even look better than you what you recall from the dive.

For overall color corrections, pink filters can help in green water, and red filters are used in blue water conditions.

Editing software also presents opportunities to improve the shot. Most modern editing programs contain tools that can manipulate a shot to achieve acceptable results. Blacks can be boosted to remove cloudiness. Exposures can be manipulated to bring out details and sharpness. Mastery of post-production and editing software is beyond the scope of this book, but will be addressed in future editions.

Color Loss

Water acts like a giant filter, removing colors as you descend. The red end of the spectrum is absorbed rather quickly in as little as 15 feet of water. The deeper you go, the more you arrive in a blue/green world, almost void of warm colors. Even in clear water, at depths of 100 feet, there is very little light penetrating through the water column, and very little color left other than indigo and blue.

Color is lost vertically in the water column but also horizontally when more filtering water is in between the camera and subject. To compensate for color and light loss, divers often carry handheld lights to restore the beauty of the natural world. Few diver-carried lights will be bright enough to illuminate the entire frame of a video shot. Instead, video lights are used to artificially provide the natural light and color of the landscape. Depending on the power of the video light, it may only be able to properly illuminate things that are close to the light source. More powerful units may have a greater ability to throw and direct light.

Water Movement

Currents, tides and surge will all affect your ability to position yourself for a shot without damaging the environment. Practice hovering in moving water and get used to drifting with the current, without getting too close to coral and other marine life.

High, slack tide tends to offer the best shooting conditions for visibility. Low tide may bring shore particulate into the water, where high tide brings deeper, cleaner, ocean water towards shore.

Fresh versus Saltwater

Excellent subjects are available in both fresh and saltwater environments. You can also shoot on the boat; half submerged or catch an action shot of divers entering the water.

The main difference between shooting in fresh or saltwater will be the buoyancy of your camera. You may need to add small trim weights for salt water. Even a very small stainless washer may be enough to trim the relative position of the camera in the water.

Camera care is even more important in saltwater, since even a small flood in saltwater can result in complete loss of the camera.

In between dives, it is best to keep the camera submerged in a tub of freshwater so that salt crystals do not dry on the buttons or lens port. If you don't have a rinse tank available, consider bringing a large Rubbermaid© tub or Pelican© case. If the boat is small, then simply wrap the camera in a damp towel.

Take great care when sharing a rinse tub with other photographers. It is in these shared tubs that most lens port scratches occur. It is also the place where the housing is most fragile. When a diver descends, the seals on the housing are improved with added pressure. In rinse tubs, the camera is not under pressure, and a latch may be opened more easily, resulting in a flood.

Interacting with Aquatic Life

Learning about how to approach a variety of marine life enhances the enjoyment of underwater videography. Open circuit divers already know that their bubbles tend to alarm fish and marine mammals. Awkward, fast motions will also startle marine life. If you spend your dive chasing things around a reef, you will likely end up with a collection of shots of fish butts. However, if you patiently stake out one location, the marine life may get used to your presence and allow you to capture a magical sequence. Macro shooters with patience will find that tiny animals like Christmas Tree Worms will come back out of their calcareous home, if they wait patiently for a few minutes without creating any unusual motions. Some animals react with great curiosity to visual stimuli, while others will retreat from unusual water movement, smell or sound.

There are many unique subjects available to shoot at night. Nocturnal animals may not even be visible until well after dark. One of the challenges of night shooting is to select the right kind of light for diving. Large video lights may attract small worms and fish that cloud the ability to get a good shot. Bright lights may also startle nocturnal creatures. Lights with multiple power settings may be helpful.

What to Shoot

The underwater world offers an abundance of subject matter. If you enjoy learning about the small occupants of the reef, then macro shooting may be very appealing. If you glory at the wonder of a sheer coral wall, then wide-angle may fit your interest. Wrecks and caves offer a never-ending maze of attractions, but remember the benefits of using a model. Models give a large area, (like a wreck or cave) a sense of scale. Models also help viewers to picture themselves in the environment. They deliver a sense of wonder and connection with human accomplishment.

Conservation

The creed among conscientious divers is to take only pictures and leave only bubbles, thus protecting the natural beauty of our underwater world. Videographers should be the very best ambassadors of the environment and should not damage anything for the sake of a photo. This includes physical damage as well as harassment of marine life. One of the greatest objectives of underwater videography is to share a magical world with those that have not had an opportunity to see these rare environments for themselves. As such, it is incumbent on the shooter to be the very best steward of the environment, and improve their diving skills and abilities to their highest level to best protect and sustain the fragile underwater ecosystem.

Beyond the Reef

Conservation of the underwater environment includes many facets. Biological life, cultural assets, geology, and historical artifacts all deserve to be left as they were found. This includes some items you may not have considered like:

Shipwrecks: They are not only historic artifacts but also precious habitat. As artificial reefs, they may find their greatest calling.

Caves: Delicate speleothems found in submerged cave systems were originally formed when the caves were dry. If broken, these beautiful formations will be forever lost. But, geological formations like rocks, clay banks and sand dunes should also be preserved. They are a part of a unique environment.

Cultural Artifacts: I have been fortunate enough to discover many items of cultural significance. It is imperative that these items be left completely undisturbed. A silt deposit in the eye socket of a skull could yield important information about how long it was submerged. Layers of leaves and detritus may give crucial evidence to a scientist. Never touch or reposition these items for the sake of a photo or critical data will be lost. Never ask a model to pick up or hold an artifact unless he/she is a scientist on a mission. This type of footage can never be used because it propagates poor behavior.

Technical Issues

Video Signals – What's in a Name?

It is time to delve into the nitty gritty of video geekdom: file formats. There are no fun and exciting stories here, just the facts!

You've likely come across .avi and .mov, but what about terms like codec, bit rate, aspect ratio and sample rate? Even if you own a seemingly simple GoPro, you'll find 1080P and 4k listed in the resolution menu. Which one should you use? What do they mean? This short section begins to unravel some of the tricky concepts found in video file formats and will help you gain a better understanding of how they all fit together. By understanding file formats, you will be able to select the right resolution for shooting and play back on different devices.

File Formats

A large amount of data is embedded in a given video signal. It is a whole lot more complicated than a simple still photo file. The information contained in a video signal includes visual material, audio attributes, dimensional information and frame rates. The data is put together in a structured container and that is called a file format. Examples are .mov or .avi. The problem with video file formats is that they don't tell you much about the quality of the product inside the container. The .mov file format might contain low quality web content or it might be far more sophisticated and hold 3D big-screen resolution with six channels of surround sound. To understand quality we need to look deeper into nomenclature.

To understand the details inside the file format container, we can review the anatomy. The file can be divided into parts including video signal, audio data and something called a codec, which refers to the software language that is used to describe the video signal. Video applications have to call on that codec to read and write the file itself.

A Question of Character

Every video file also has certain characteristics. These attributes include things like frame size, aspect ratio, frame rate, bit rate and audio sample rate. Let's look at these individually.

Frame Size refers to the actual dimensions of pixels that make up the image. This is commonly called "resolution," since a lot of pixels are needed to make up the sharpest, high-resolution image. Your GoPro camera offers resolutions up to 4K, which is actually 3940 × 2160 pixels. The popular 1080 resolution is made up of a frame size of 1920 x 1080 pixels.

Aspect Ratio refers to the proportional width and height of the visual material. Older television sets used to offer up an image that was 4 x 3 in dimension, expressed as 4:3. Now HD sets appear in a different shape. This is a ratio of 16:9. Your DSLR camera might shoot still photos in 3 x 2 aspect ratio. When you switch to shooting video on the same camera, you may see a dark area on the top and bottom of the 3 x 2 viewfinder on the back of the camera. It looks different than the still photo you just shot. It appears cropped. The video is often designed to shoot in 16:9 format that is common to most modern televisions. It "masks" the viewfinder to show you the new framing. This concept is referred to as letter boxing. The masked area in your viewfinder won't appear in your video, so keep that in mind as you shoot.

Frame Rate is almost like a shutter speed. The package that is the video file is essentially comprised of a whole bunch of still images recorded in fractions of seconds in rapid succession. The human brain is able to smooth rapid images into a continuous stream through a concept called "persistence of vision." If you have ever watched an old black and white Charlie Chaplain film, you've seen a slow frame rate that makes the footage appear jumpy. Our brains can begin to make a smooth stream at about 8 frames per second (fps), but does a much better job starting around 24 fps. Movies in your local cinema are displayed at 24 fps and appear "dreamier" than faster frame rates seen in modern television. Commonly we see 60 fps as the standard rate for 720p HD and 30 fps on broadcast television in North America and other countries that use the NTSC (National Television System Committee) set of video standards. In Europe, you'll see 25 fps on broadcast TV, since they use the PAL (Phase Alternating Line) set of standards. More correctly, the frame rates are actually expressed with fractions of frames as 29.97 instead of 30 and 23.98 instead of 24 fps. These fractions arose from the distribution methods of modern television, when engineers were challenged with transmitting color television broadcast signals through the power grid. Engineers had to slow down the video frame by a fraction of a percent for compatibility reasons.

Bit Rate refers to how much data describes the video or audio portion of the file. This is measured in units per second as kilobytes (kb), megabytes (mb) or gigabytes (gb). The higher the bit rate, the better the quality of the material.

Audio Sample Rate is an additional figure that tells us how often the actual audio is sampled when it is converted into digital information.

Reviewing Quality

With this information in mind, let's revisit the popular GoPro camera. The 4k setting on the Hero4 Black is able to record 30 fps. The older model only offered 12 fps. You could use that for excellent time-lapse footage by speeding it up in the edit suite, but the frame rate was generally too low for smooth video display. With upgraded 4K 30 fps, it is a huge leap forward, but the GoPro convenience means it will always have a really tiny sensor. That's why the retail price is around $500 and a professional 4K camera could set you back $15,000 for the body alone. HD is not all alike. Larger sensors can record more information, are capable of more dynamic range, have less noise and better low light capability.

Chart: Relative frame dimensions of several standard video formats.

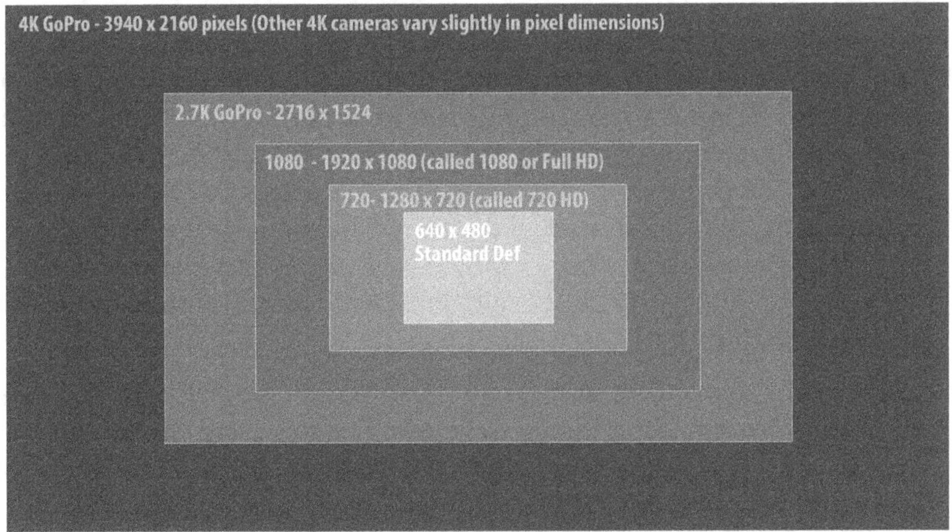

Making an Artistic Choice

If you want to give your underwater footage that dreamy appearance of a motion picture or produce it on DVD, Blu-Ray or the Internet, then 24 fps is your best selection. If you plan on broadcasting on television, then you should record at 30 (29.97) fps in North America or the PAL standard 25 fps for Europe. If you want the sweet spot of quality with manageable file sizes, then 1080 at a higher frame rate will give you great quality and the option to run footage in slow speeds.

Card Games

Choosing the Right Memory Card for Your Camera

Digital cameras use a removable storage device in the form of a memory card in order to store your video and photo files. When you tear open the box of a new camera, you sometimes need to temper your excitement. That new camera may not include a memory card, which means delayed gratification and yes, spending a few more dollars before you can use your new device.

Flash memory cards use solid-state technology, meaning that there are no moving parts inside the plastic case. Although all memory cards serve the same general purpose, there are proprietary formats and attributes you should understand before running off to the discount store to buy the least expensive card you can find.

The good news for divers is that memory cards are very durable. They are generally waterproof and can usually withstand immersion in salt and freshwater. As long as the card is fully dried and cleaned before use, it will operate as normal after it has been flooded underwater or been exposed to moisture in places such as a wet countertop, damp cup holder or in the rain. The same technology is very temperature resilient, shockproof, X-ray proof and basically able to be run over by a 5-ton delivery truck. (Not tested by this writer, but on my husband's list).

In general, Secure Digital (SD) and CompactFlash (CF) are the most common formats. Most new consumer cameras use the smaller SD format while larger, professional and prosumer cameras often use CompactFlash or both simultaneously. A few cameras are able to facilitate multiple formats and some utilize proprietary configurations such s Sony's Memory Stick. The camera manufacturer will specify the size and type of memory card, but beyond format, there is a literal minefield of features to consider when purchasing a card.

Compatibility

In the SD family of cards, you will find SD, SD High Capacity (SDHC) and the most recent Extended Capacity (SDXC) types. Most devices made in the last five years will likely accept SDHC and very new cameras will use SDXC. Cameras can use older cards, but older cameras may not be able to use newer formats. SD cards are also made in three physical sizes for different sized cameras - SD, miniSD and microSD.

Understanding Card Speed

All memory cards are marked with symbols and language that define their speed, which is further divided into write speed and read speed. Write speed is particularly critical for burst shooting and video applications, while read speed is noticeable when downloading images to your computer.

Cards may be described with a multiplication factor that indicates read speed (200x, 300x, etc.). This is called the "Commercial X Rating." A 200x rated card is equivalent to 200 times the speed of an original CD-ROM, which ran at 150 KB/sec. Therefore a 200x card would read a 29.5 MB image file in one second (200 x 150 = 30,000/1016 = 29.528). More recently, the SD Association devised a speed class rating which describes the minimum data transfer rate of SD/SDHC/SDXC cards. Class 4 cards will perform 4 MB/sec; Class 10 cards reach 10 MB/sec., and so on. This is important for video recording so that the card can keep up with the data stream pouring out of the video camera.

In a nutshell, purchase the fastest card you can afford.

A photographer may be happy with a Class 4 card, but a video shooter should look for a Class 6 card if their camera supports it. Read the manufacturer's recommendations to be sure you are not overspending on something that will operate slower in an older camera.

The storage capacity of the card is described in GB. Although you may be tempted to buy a large capacity, don't use this as an excuse to retain two years worth of footage and photos before you download to a computer. Store only as much as you are willing to lose. Most cards are specified with a Mean Time Before Failure (MTBF) of over 100 years but occasional failures or physical loss are not unheard of.

CF cards are rated with transfer speed, which is the highest possible read speed, but bear in mind that the rating on the SD card indicates minimum write speed. When tested, many SDHC and SDXC cards tend to deliver 20-30 MB/sec (133-200x) and have potential write speeds of 80 MB/sec and are gaining speed all the time.

Maintaining Your Card

When you finish your day of underwater shooting, take time to off-load your sequences to your computer or other device. Once you have completed this task, reformat the card in the camera to minimize errors and increase speed. If you are using a GoPro or similar camera and don't reformat, at least "empty the trash" on your computer to ensure availability of the full capacity of the card. Remember that formatting a card will irretrievably erase files, so ensure they are backed up first.

So, after the joy of unboxing a new camera, take a moment to decide which card will work best for you. Consult the instructional manual to ensure you are not purchasing more card than you can handle. Turn your focus to the capacity and speed that best fits the camera and your budget and stick to a known and reliable brand.

Focus Pocus

You've just completed a lengthy dive off the Cayman Wall and shot breathtaking video of a variety of gorgeous creatures along the reef. Relying on auto focus worked out fairly well and you are sure you have canned some awe-inspiring, colorful footage. Hanging on the deco bar under the boat, you are presented with the opportunity of a lifetime. A behemoth manta ray swims towards you from out of the blue, its cephalic lobes outstretched and reaching towards you as it glides through the deep open water. Trembling with excitement, you quickly bring your video camera up to your face and press record. The manta swims in arcs around you, attempting to shake off its friendly remora travelers. Your exposure looks terrific and you giggle over the footage that is bound to represent one of the best moments of your diving career. Yet, after the exhilaration has passed and you have a moment to review your work, you discover that your footage is less than perfect. It appears to be in focus one moment and then attempting to keep your amazing subject sharp and clear, the lens ratchets in and out softening the next frames. An ebb and flow of focus coming and going has ruined the shot. What could possibly have gone wrong?

Shooting a large pelagic out in the deep blue open water offers unique challenges. The environment is both low in contrast and available light. There is generally a lot of filtering blue water between you and the biggest creatures of the sea. If your camera is set in auto focus, it will randomly alternate between acceptable sharpness and a fuzzy image as the lens elements automatically shift back and forth, focusing on particles in the water, then the animal, then the water column again, unable to find its mark. The camera needs contrast to lock in focus effectively and this underwater environment lacks contrast.

There are several great strategies for preparing to capture as much sharply focused footage as possible. If you have a zoom lens on your camera, set it at the widest angle possible. Preset the focus on something within the range of three to five feet. You can do this on the boat or focus on your own fin once you jump in the water. After you are confident with the focus, set the camera to lock the focus in place.

I like to check that this all works prior to jumping in the water. Some cameras can be placed in their housing with the focus button in the wrong position, rendering the housing switch unusable. If you check before you jump, you'll avoid disappointment.

Many video cameras are equipped with a sticky switch that allows the diver to momentarily slip into auto focus. If something interests you within close range, you simply rock the switch to grab the auto focus and then allow it to fall back into the manual locked position again. Once you start shooting a subject that is more distant you simply rock the switch again to grab auto focus and lock. Other housing models toggle between manual and auto focus. When you hit the focus switch, these cameras operate in auto focus. If you hit the switch a second time, the camera will operate in manual, but locked, focus. Continuous manual focus on the fly is a really difficult skill and rarely nets the best results. Most underwater viewfinders do not offer adequate resolution to empower you to accurately focus while swimming.

Wide-angle lenses or lenses zoomed out to the widest view; offer the greatest depth of field. They provide the additional advantage of permitting you to get very close to your subject, thus reducing the amount of light and color filtering water between you and your subject. Many shooters choose to lock focus at the beginning of dive and shoot almost anything between two to three feet and infinity and net great results.

HDSLR cameras, such as the Canon 5D Mkii, present some additional challenges when it comes to focus. Very few high-end HDSLR cameras offer any continuous auto focus capability at all while in video mode. Many HDSLR housings have an auto focus button that can grab focus and lock it. Unfortunately, it can be almost painful waiting for the camera to find sharpness and sometimes the camera will erroneously choose to focus on some barely seen particle in the water, rendering the entire shot soft. The best advice for these types of cameras is to select something with as high-contrast as possible or clearly definable edges. When the camera attempts to focus on stripes or hard edges, it generally locks focus much faster and more accurately. Once you have achieved auto lock, then make a mental note of the distance to your subject. Everything within that range will also be sharp as well as a significant range in front of and behind the subject. It is only when you choose to shoot very close subjects, less than three feet away, that you will need to hit the auto lock button again. Adding an expanded viewfinder or small HD monitor will make operating and focusing an HDSLR camera much easier.

Some video cameras do not offer a focus button at all. Compact video cameras, GoPro POV cameras and inexpensive point-and-shoot cameras often only have auto focus capability. Auto focus cameras are improving exponentially all the time, but to achieve best results with these simple video cameras, hold them steady and try not to bounce around between subjects at different distances from your position. Shoot long segments, understanding that the camera needs a few moments to find and process ideal sharpness. Count to five after your subject has passed to complete your shot. Consider that low contrast subjects swimming in blue water without a background are going to be very difficult to capture.

When you begin to master all the options for focusing your camera, you'll be a better prepared and confident underwater videographer when you are face to face with one of a diver's greatest encounters - a manta ray or whale shark in the deep blue sea.

Depth of Field

Depth of Field is the distance between the nearest and farthest objects in a scene that appear acceptably sharp in an image. When you are shooting video, a large depth of field is often called deep focus and a small depth is field is known as shallow focus. If you are shooting a moving animal, deep focus, or a large depth of field is helpful.

Focus Peaking Features

Many higher-end video cameras offer a feature called focus peaking. With this feature activated, the edges of things that are in focus are highlighted with a color such as green. The feature helps the shooter focus when using a small viewfinder or LCD display.

Here is a video link to help you understand some of the pros and cons of focus peaking: https://www.youtube.com/watch?v=jMAl-MQev7Kw

Histograms

When I first transitioned to digital cameras, I was disappointed that footage shot underwater in the cave looked excellent on the screen, but was terribly underexposed when downloaded to my computer. The LCD screen can lure you into thinking you have a great shot, especially when viewed in low-light conditions. With a good understanding of a feature called histograms, you will get a much higher percentage of well-exposed shots.

The histogram is actually a metering function of the camera, which is viewed on the LCD screen. As a matter of practice, the LCD photo image should only be used to evaluate composition, whereas the histogram should be used to critique exposure. Some cameras can display a histogram on top of the image during shooting and others display the histogram only upon review.

One of the considerations of exposure is contrast, or the range of tones between the lightest and darkest areas of a photograph. Many people are familiar with contrast controls on television and computer screens.

Traditional photographic film could only provide an acceptable exposure in the range of a few f-stops. Today's digital camera sensors can record a larger range of acceptable light, considered to be around five or six f-stops. Some high contrast underwater scenes may contain a range of 10 or 12 f-stops of light.

How to Read Histograms

A histogram is a bar graph that shows you 256 brightness levels for your image from pure black on the left to pure white on the right. It also allows you to see the distribution of tones in an image. The taller the peak of a bar on the graph, the more of that particular tone, you will see in the photo. The more pixels you see on the right, the brighter the image. The more pixels you see on the left, the darker the image. An underexposed shot will show all the pixels piled

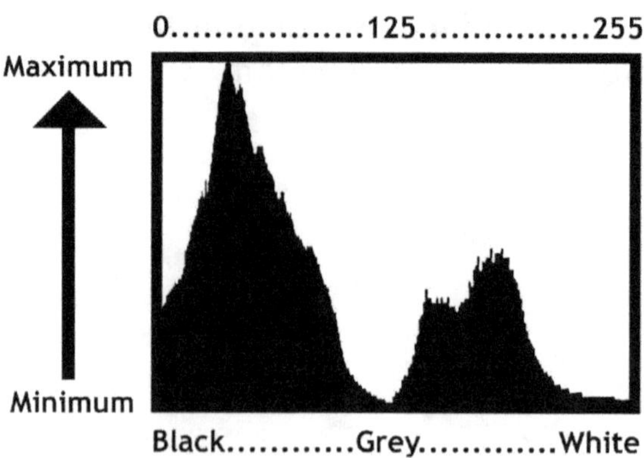

on the left of the graph and an overexposed shot will show all the pixels piled on the right. A flat looking sequence will have all the pixels bunched in the middle. A contrasty photo will have tall peaks on each end of the histogram.

When we review a histogram, we concentrate mainly on the far left and far right. If bars fill up the left of the screen and peak at the top, then critical information has been lost. You cannot lighten the darkest area to recover detail if the histogram peaks on the left. The converse is true on the right side. If the bars fill up the right side and peak at the top, then there are areas of complete whiteness without any detail remaining. When the right or left side of the histogram is filled to the top of the graph, we call this "clipping."

Well-distributed peaks and valleys allow for a lot of adjustment in image editing programs, although a histogram does not need to cover an entire window. An underwater cave image should not clip on the left, but most of the data will still fill the left side of the bar graph since this dark blue environment does not contain all the colors of the spectrum.

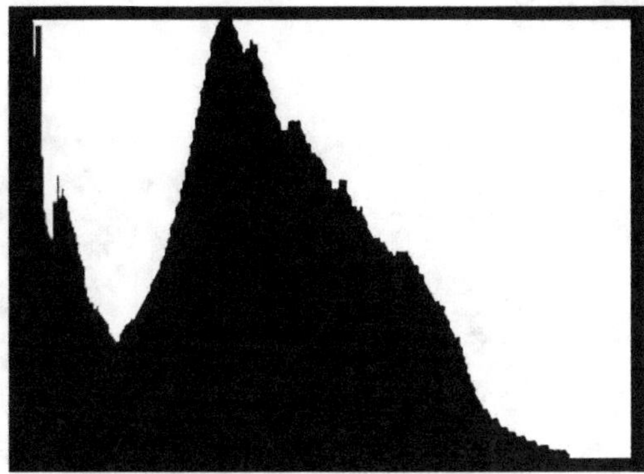

A Histogram Representing an Underexposed Shot

Using Histograms Underwater to Make Adjustments

Many digital cameras offer several viewing options on the LCD screen. The full frame screen is a good tool for composition and a reasonable judge for serious focusing errors. The "highlight" screen, available on some cameras, will flicker the area where white has been clipped from the image or provide "zebra stripes" where images are close to clipping range.

The human eye is not very forgiving to an image with blown-out white areas or highlights, but understands better, an image with dark, clipped shadow areas. We call dark photos artistic and moody but clipped highlights are considered overexposed mistakes. Refer to the histogram screen after your shot and quickly scan it for clipping on either end. Exposure and composition adjustments can then be made to improve the next shot.

Exposure adjustments can be made in several ways. In manual mode, the f-stop or shutter speed can be adjusted. Light can also be added or subtracted using the camera's exposure compensation button (EV +/-). So, even if you have chosen to shoot using automatic modes, you can tweak the settings after reviewing the histogram.

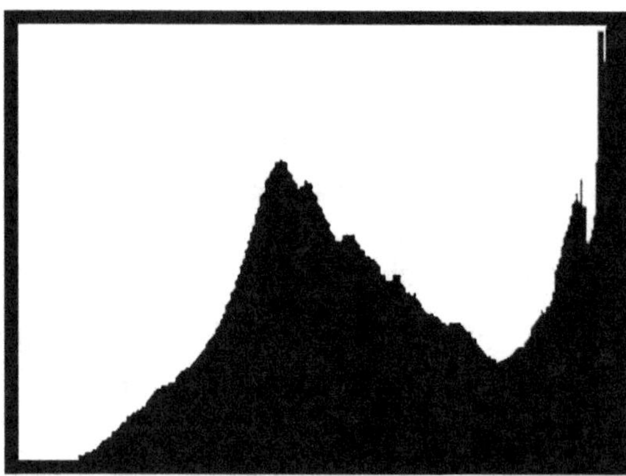

Once you have mastered using histograms, you can use them to create a very unique "look" for your photos and return from every dive with well-exposed shots that can be improved in image-editing programs.

A Histogram Representing an Overexposed Shot

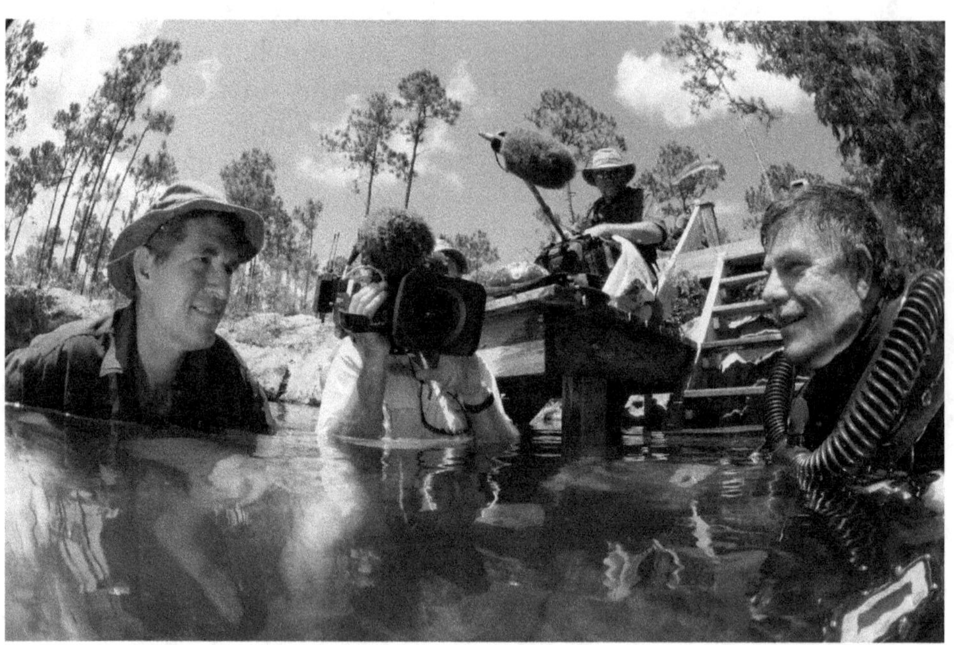

Filming PBS NOVA in Abaco, Bahamas.

Ten Tips for Shooting Great Underwater Video

Whether you are a new shooter or a sage professional, here are ten quick tips to improve your underwater video.

Preparation

1. Practice in a pool.

With any new camera, it is just as important to get a sense of the weight and balance of a system as well as get familiar with all the controls. Take your new camera on a pool dive to test the buoyancy and help you make decisions about how to manage the rig. The test dive will also give you comfort that everything works and there are no leaks. If your lighting arms feel unmanageable, consider purchasing a neutrally buoyant set from Ultralight Control Systems. If the housing is too buoyant, then use carefully placed trim weights to even out the unit (these trim weights may need to be shifted or increased in salt water). Consider how you will hold the system with one hand in the event that your other hand is needed for buoyancy adjustments, ear clearing and hanging on a line.

Shooting

2. Get as close to your subject as possible.

Use a wide-angle lens and dome. If you are using a zoom lens, then zoom out to the widest field of view. Move in as close as possible to your subject to reduce the amount of light- and color-filtering water between you and your subject. Color, contrast and sharpness are all improved by moving close to your subject.

3. Learn to look at light.

Spend an entire dive on a single subject. Shoot it from different angles so that you can get a feel for the different qualities of light. When the sun illuminates an object from the side, it provides hard edges that contribute to a sense of space. Illuminating an object from behind or backlighting with the sun can create a silhouette. An object illuminated from the front has a completely different feel.

4. Take your finger off the zoom.

It is far better to swim to your subject than use the zoom button. If you watch good underwater programming, you will rarely see an underwater zoom shot. If you do, it is very slow and steady.

Workflow

5. Buy the best memory card you can afford.

Purchase a backup card for the second dive of the day. Memory cards are inexpensive compared to your camera setup and travel to a destination. If your card size matches or exceeds your dive time, then you will be able to roll through the bulk of the dive and you'll never miss an important moment. You can break long sequences into more manageable sized clips later on and discard footage that did not meet your expectations. Memory cards need to be "ultra" or "fast" rated to handle the demands of video (see earlier section - Card Games).

6. Purchase name brand batteries.

Canon, Sony and other name brand batteries are made specifically for their specific camera systems. There are always cheap knock-offs available online that promise equal quality but rarely net the results. If you use the correct batteries and chargers for your camera system, your batteries will last longer and rarely leave you disappointed on a dive.

Manufacturers have very specific recommendations in regards to rechargeable batteries in their lighting systems. Heed their warnings. Some batteries get very hot and may create an over-pressurization in the battery compartment of your light. If this happens, you'll end up flooding your instrument. It's a lot cheaper to purchase and use the correct batteries for the gear.

Editing

7. Watch quality television programs.

Tune into BBC documentaries, Discovery Channel programs and National Geographic Specials. Analyze their editing techniques to reveal what it takes to craft a cohesive story. List the types of shots you have seen, such as close-ups, master shots and point-of-view (POV) shots and examine how long each shot remains on the screen. Note how the cameraman holds the shot steady without bouncing around too much. Try to find a few shots that you would like to emulate in your own unique environment.

8. Shoot the context.

Remember to shoot sequences of people on the boat and jumping into the water. Every video needs establishing shots to glue it all together. Shoot the entry sign at the dive shop or the chalkboard with the day's dive site. Shoot the Divemaster loading tanks or the Captain talking on the radio. Get some shots of your team assembling their equipment or a close-up of the SPG as they turn on the tank. You will use every one of these cutaway shots in your edit and always wish you had more.

Travel

9. Bring your own dunk tank.

When traveling with a large duffle bag, place a lightweight Rubbermaid© or similar brand bin inside the duffle. This will help protect your dive gear in transit and double as a private rinse tank once you arrive at your destination. Many camera floods happen in dive boat dunk tanks. Too may people crowd their systems into one big bin. They slosh around on the bouncing deck and cause floods and scratches to dome ports. If there is not enough water on the boat to fill your private bin, then place a towel over the system to keep it moist. Rinse and soak the entire system well when the dock gets back to the dock.

Insurance

10. Insure you camera system.

There are excellent options for insuring your camera system. Some homeowner policies will cover a loss by theft, but you may need to list the system with the insurer as a separate line item. If your home policy does not cover you, then purchase insurance from a company such as Senn and Dunn through the Divers Alert Network. Their insurance is available to DAN members as an additional policy. The purchaser lists specific items that they wish to insure and places a value on each. The premium is calculated based on the total value of the gear. In the event of a loss by theft or lost luggage, the declared value is refunded without a deductible. In the event of a flood, then the full repair or declared value is refunded less a ten percent deductible. If you drop your camera off the dive boat and it is not recovered, then there is no coverage. It seems like a very fair policy and I have had great interactions with the staff and easy refunds for loss.

The Art of Videography

Composition

Composition is the artistry in your work and it refers to how elements are arranged and move through a frame. As such, composition can be very subjective. What is beautiful to one individual may not be as pleasing to another viewer. Even with the subjective realities of art appreciation, there are some general rules that will aid in creating beautiful compositions.

There are seven basic elements of composition that are pleasing to the human eye. They are described below.

Path

The human eye needs to be able to move around the frame of the shot. Visual elements that point the viewer's attention around the frame are pleasing. A diver looking at a fish in profile allows the viewer's eye to dance from the diver to the fish and back within the frame. A fish swimming away from the lens confers a disturbing feeling of retreat.

The subject in motion needs room to move within the frame. If they are in the corner of the picture swimming off the edge of the photo, it will leave the viewer feeling disjointed. If the camera tracks with the motion with room for the subject to move within the frame it is far better than uncomfortable cropping.

All that aside, it is fine for a subject to enter the frame on one side and exit on the other. In these shots, the fish or diver enters and exits frame comfortably, but leave enough tail on the end of the shot to permit cuts and transitions in the edit.

Shape

Geometric and organic shapes are created in a photograph by the arrangement of objects. Sometimes they can have unintended consequences on the photo. When shooting a diver head-on, sometimes their fins appear as though they are coming out of their head. This posture may represent good diving technique that prevents the fins from contact with the reef, but the appearance of this posture makes the diver look like they have Mickey Mouse ears. If the model is asked to rotate their position to a slight profile, the resulting line and shape may create a beautiful diagonal leading line through the picture.

Color

Color is often associated with different moods. Soft muted colors may evoke peacefulness, where boldly contrasted colors may be considered brash. Colors that oppose each other on the color wheel tend to be very pleasing. The underwater world is so blue that when a diver wears red or orange, it is quite strikingly beautiful.

Black and white shots can have their own special allure. With access to modern editing equipment, it is always better to shoot your video clean, in full color and then translate the sequence to black and white during post-processing. Black and white is excellent for vintage subjects like shipwrecks or historical sequences.

Texture

The patterns on a surface create may be used to evoke tactile sensations. Orderly patterns found in the undersea world, like coral polyps or sea fans, may give a pleasing sense of order to a shot. Contrasting textures may be very appealing as in shots that have textures displayed in the foreground and soft focus in the background.

Size

The relative size of one object to another can give a very different result. A large foreground shark with a tiny diver in the background will make the viewer uneasy about the safety of a diver. The reverse shot of a large foreground diver viewing a smaller background shark will give a completely different feel. With a shark in the foreground and a small diver in the background, a cameraman can track alongside the two subjects as they swim along a reef.

Perspective

Perspective is the illusion of depth. A sequence with a discernible foreground, middle and background will have depth and will naturally draw the viewer's interest. Always look to layer your shots with numerous elements if possible. You can peak through the kelp at a Garibaldi or track alongside a diver that is partially obscured by a submerged tree. It is gives the viewer the sense that they are passive viewers on a secret world.

Space

Some objects appear as positive items and the empty area in between is perceived as negative space. The balance between negative and positive space will affect how the viewer feels about a shot.

Artistry

The artistry and unique aspects of a shot are created by experimenting with the seven elements of design. The right combination can create a harmonious, pleasing sequence that may be judged as beautiful. A different combination could result in a photograph that is deemed disturbing or jarring. Even with excellent exposure, a diver whose head is cut off the edge of the shot will not win any awards.

When using a model, the photographer has the opportunity to select how the viewer should interact with the diver. If the camera viewpoint looks straight down on a diver in a bait ball with sharks, he may seem vulnerable. If the angle of the photo looks up at the diver who fills the frame while he feeds the sharks, this may leave more of an impression of power and control.

The Rule of Thirds

You have carefully used your hard earned savings to book the dive trip of a lifetime and have painstakingly prepared your underwater video system to capture that elusive manta or majestic whale shark. *Knowing where* to place those subjects in the viewfinder can be as important as spotting them in the first place. The unique intuition involved in good composition and proportion can be the difference between a routine video of your underwater experience or a breathtaking visual experience that you can be proud to share with the world on You Tube or Vimeo. Luckily, you can practice good composition techniques every time you dive and in any conditions. Using your dive buddies as underwater models, you can experiment with directing how they move through the frame of your viewfinder and learn to develop a sense of good composition.

The foundation for outstanding composition in art, photography and videography comes from a basic mathematical principle witnessed in nature. This concept is called the Rule of Thirds. You might have noticed that the viewfinder of your camera offers an option that displays a grid in the frame of reference, dividing it into a tic-tac-toe board with nine cells. By dividing the viewfinder into three columns and three rows, it creates four intersection points where the lines cross inside the frame. The Rule of Thirds tells us that the points of the intersecting lines are the most interesting to the human brain. If your general composition is divided into elements that fall into the thirds, then the action, or strongest area of interest should take place at the intersecting points, with the motion moving into the frame. In underwater shooting, that gives the subject, such as the fish or the diver, room to naturally swim into the field of the picture rather than falling out of the edges of the composition. If your subject is constantly pressing against the forward edge of the frame, it is disturbing and seems compositionally "off balanced."

Almost everything in our natural world follows this pattern of design. Whether it is a star nebula or chambered Nautilus shell, these elegantly designed works of nature illustrate the Rule of Thirds. As such, it is generally accepted that the human mind finds peace and pleasure in things that follow the golden rules of composition in the natural world. If you examine the human face, it is naturally divided into thirds. The faces of most attractive models fit tightly within this format. You may have noticed that the Rule of Thirds applies in the most pleasing art, architecture and even web site design.

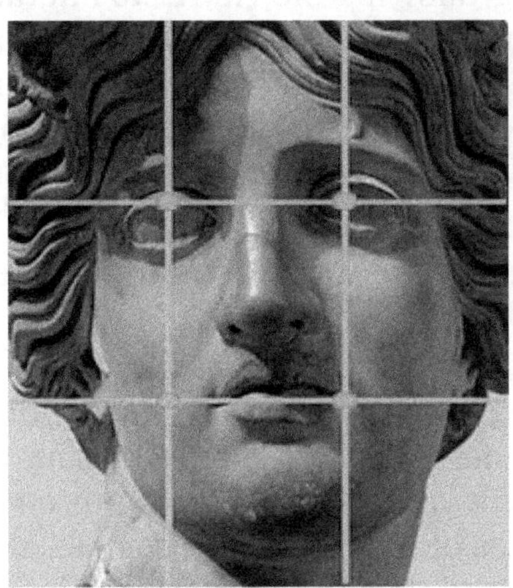

This classic roman sculpture shows how our perception of a beautiful face is based on proportion that falls into a grid of thirds.

The human eye rarely rests. Our minds process visual information by bouncing around and grabbing visual snippets of information. If we organize a composition in a way that allows the human brain to follow a logical path to process information, it will be more pleasing. If you simply place your subject in the center of your frame, it is considered bland and static. The viewer's eye gets drawn to the center of the shot and has no obvious clue about where to go next. With the border of visual information around the subject equal on every side, the viewer's eye rests on the center and stays there. This may work for a head shot of a news anchor, but only if the audio content they are reporting is interesting enough to hold the observer's attention. If you watch the news, you'll notice that the news anchor is often placed in one third of the frame with a live action video window in another third of the shot. The anchor's eyes lead the viewer to the inserted video pane. When you are communicating with visual information only, as is often with underwater videography, then you need to be creative to stimulate the viewer's attention. By positioning the subject on one of the intersecting points in the Rule of Thirds, it forces the viewer's eye to roam to find the primary point of interest. If you allow the subject to move diagonally through the frame from one intersection to another, then the viewer's brain will track with the subject, permitting the illusion of three dimensions. Your video will be more captivating, allowing the viewer to interact and feel like they are participating in the dive. This type of shooting facilitates a shared experience between the videographer and the viewer.

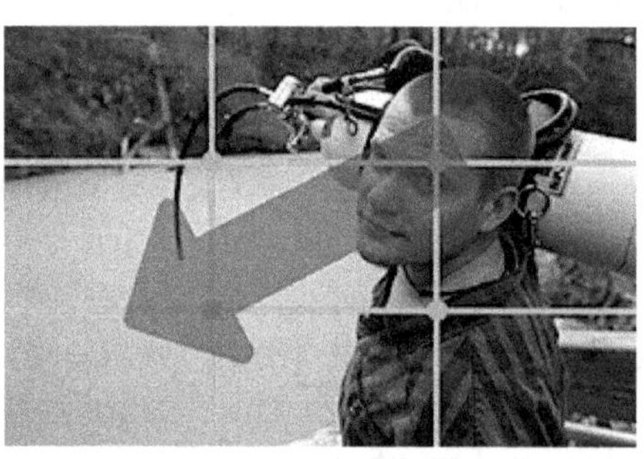

When filming your buddies as they prepare for a dive, start your shot with attention to the intersections in the Rule of Thirds allowing action to move through the frame to a diagonal counterpoint.

When filming a subject such as a wreck or a reef, you can position your background so that it flows along the horizontal division of cells in the Rule of Thirds, then shoot your models moving through the intersection points either towards or away from the camera. You can also use the lines of a wreck to lead the viewer's eyes on a diagonal path through the intersections of the Rule of Thirds. When filming a close-up shot with a model, position the models eyes in one-third of the screen looking down onto a subject in an intersecting point on the opposing third of the frame. By placing the primary focal point (the model's eyes) in a thirds position, you will be enhancing the photo with a counterpoint in the diagonal position (the close-up subject, such as an anemone) that gives the eye and imagination a place to roam.

The Rule of Thirds is one of the most important things to learn when you start shooting. It's the basis for pleasing, well-balanced and interesting shots. This formula will give you a good compositional foundation allowing for further creativity and exciting footage that sets you apart from the average underwater shooter.

In a medium shot, this instructor's eyes and attention are focused on the other diver's equipment leading the viewer's imagination to fill in the blanks about an instructor helping a student.

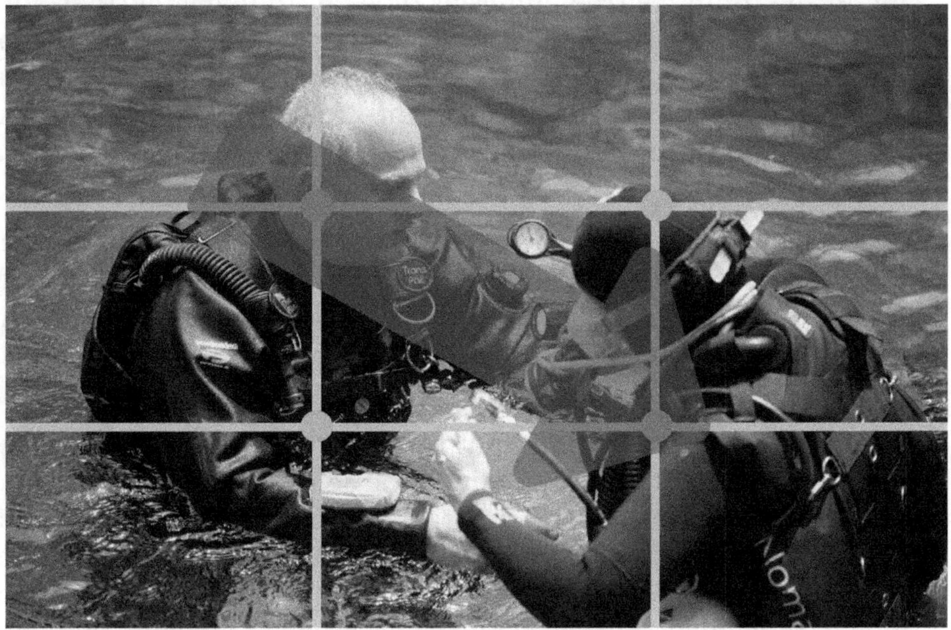

The Rule of Odds

This rule suggests that an odd number of subjects in a shot are more pleasing than an even number of items. This stems from the organization of the Rule of Thirds. Thus, if you have more than one diver in a shot, it will be more pleasing to see three, rather than two. In this light, triangles are also pleasing negative or positive spaces within a shot. The human face is essentially an equilateral triangle from the eyes to the mouth. As a result, our minds find balance in that shape.

Limiting Depth of Field

Limiting the focal range in a photo will bring attention to the object in focus. Our eyes are naturally attracted to the compositional element that is in sharpest focus. This technique can be used to draw the eye into a particular item or quadrant of a shot. This simplification makes the viewing experience "easy" and therefore pleasurable.

Language of the Shot

According to the theory of left-brain or right-brain dominance, each side of the brain controls different types of thinking. Furthermore, people are said to favor one type of thinking over the other. A person who is "left-brained" is often said to be more logical, analytical and objective, while a person who is "right-brained" is said to be more intuitive, thoughtful and subjective. This represents the practical versus the creative.

Video editing is an activity that requires two distinctly different talents. Organizational skills are just as important as artistic virtuosity. The best editors maintain a happy balance between the left and right hemispheres of their brains.

Considering that traditional documentary films are often shot at a ratio of ten to one, meaning that for every minute of final footage, ten minutes are left for the archives, the sensible editor must simultaneously make critical and creative decisions regarding the final version of their work. I have been involved in projects that utilized over 200 unique tapes shot over the course of several years. It's one thing to remember shooting a particular scene or element, but being able to find it in the mass of media on tapes and hard drives can be challenging. More importantly you need to ensure you have shot all the critical elements in the first place. There are times when I have searched for hours for a much-needed video element, only to discover, to my dismay that it simply wasn't shot. I've also been convinced that I captured a certain scene on video, when actually, I shot stills with my DSLR. This is when my competing brain hemispheres give me an editing headache.

If you analyze your favorite television show, you will find that there are many different types of shots that make up a final edited program. A single unique shot may be on the screen for several seconds or just in the wink of an eye. Editors cut from one type of shot to the next, allowing the viewer to experience many different viewpoints that make up a story. More importantly, editing accelerates us through time, creating a visual montage that moves the story forward.

There is a secret language used to describe particular types of shots that make up an edit. Frames, shots, clips, scenes and sequences form a range of units that form a final program. Understanding this language will help you create an inventory of the types of shots that are needed for a project. If you use this language consistently, it is a great tool to help you locate particular files when you need them. I've given short acronyms to different types of shots in my organizational hierarchy to help me keep track of my irreplaceable video work.

The first essential shot is called the "master." The master shot establishes a time and place and is usually shot in a wide angle. A good master shot for your diving video might be a solid ten second run of everyone boarding the boat. In my keyword and file naming protocols, I always label a master shot "MS." For example, my file name might be "group boarding vessel MS." If you use valuable keywords to describe your individual files, you can assign terms such as "group, dive boat, topside, and dock, MS."

The next series of shot categories are labeled according to the framing of the scene. A wide shot (WS), is similar to a master shot in its field of view but isn't necessarily a sequence that fulfills the requirements of a master shot. People in the shot are usually shown head to toe and not cropped in any way. A medium shot (MED) usually shows people from the waist up. A close-up (CU) includes either head and shoulders or just a person's face. An extreme close-up (ECU) might just show an individual's teary eye or their lips as they speak. In an underwater scene a close-up may include a diver's face as they blow bubbles, where an extreme close-up could show an SPG gauge while the tank valve is turned on. Long shots (LS) are very distant from the subject. A good example of a long shot would be looking up the ascent line to a backlit group of divers silhouetted against the sun.

There is also a language for shots that include a particular type of camera motion. A "tilt up" (TU) begins level and slowly tilts upward to a stationary shot. A good example of a tilt up could be capturing the moment when someone breaks the surface, tilting up to reveal the Divemaster assisting on the back deck. This is sometimes referred to as a "reveal," since the shot begins neutral and moves upward to disclose the true subject of the shot. A "tilt down" (TD) is simply the opposite move. The shooter begins neutral, perhaps on the bubbles striking the ceiling of the wreck and then smoothly angles the camera downward to reveal a diver searching the wreck with their dive light. When the camera is moved laterally left or right, these shots are called "pans" (PAN). You should fluidly pan a camera slowly to the left or to the right. Tracking shots (TS) are one of the most challenging to capture underwater. The camera operator moves at the same speed as the subject, tracking them through a scene. In a wreck, a camera operator can swim alongside a diver while shooting them in profile as they explore the inside of the sunken vessel.

There are a few other unique techniques that will add spice to your repertoire of shots. A "Dutch tilt" is often used to portray tension or fun in the subject being filmed. This shot is achieved by tilting the camera so that the shot is composed diagonally. Most Dutch tilts are shot stationary, or with a very quick tilt that reveals the diagonal angle. The late director Alfred Hitchcock was a master of the suspenseful Dutch tilt camera position. A point of view shot (POV) places the camera in the position the viewer would see if they were a part of the scene. In a short underwater scene an edit might contain a tracking shot of a diver swimming along the reef, followed by a POV shot of what the diver might be looking at, such as a shark cutting across their path, followed by a pan of the shark swimming right to left out of the frame.

The most often overlooked shot is the very valuable "cutaway" (CA). This is the critical glue that holds an edit together. Without cutaway shots, the edit can suffer from "jump cutting." A jump cut is a situation in which two shots of the same subject in a similar frame are used in sequence. If these shots are similar in camera position that varies only slightly, then the subject of the shot will appear to jump in position in a jerky or disjointed manner. In general, it is recommend that consecutive shots should vary by at least 30 degrees of camera position or an obvious switch in framing as in from a wide shot to a close-up.

You've probably noticed temporal jump cuts in a documentary interview, when an editor slices the middle out of a sequence. This usually occurs when an editor lacks cutaway material allowing them to shift for a moment while they construct a coherent audio sequence out of many interview segments. This is among the most important reasons for shooting cutaway shots. If you shoot an interview, take some time at the end to shoot the subject's hands as they make a series of gestures. Take a close-up shot of the logo on their shirt or the diploma on the wall that shows their name. If they are speaking to someone, shoot the listener while they nod or smile or react to a sequence. With divers, you can shoot equipment prep, close-ups of people donning gear, or even the wake behind the boat. Theses short segues will help you assemble a sequence without jump cuts.

Using the "language of the shot" will help you become a better camera operator. If you are thinking ahead to the parts and pieces you will need during your editing, you'll have a much better chance of crafting a cohesive and entertaining story. You'll also increase your odds of finding that one-in-a-million critical shot from a trip you made three years ago. And, you will spare yourself the migraine headache of your left-brain confronting your right.

If you are going to tell a cohesive story, you will need a variety of shots to make up the edit. Many topside shots may be needed to tell the full narrative. In this series, two divers hike through the woods, rappel down into a sinkhole and discover human remains that they retrieve for a museum.

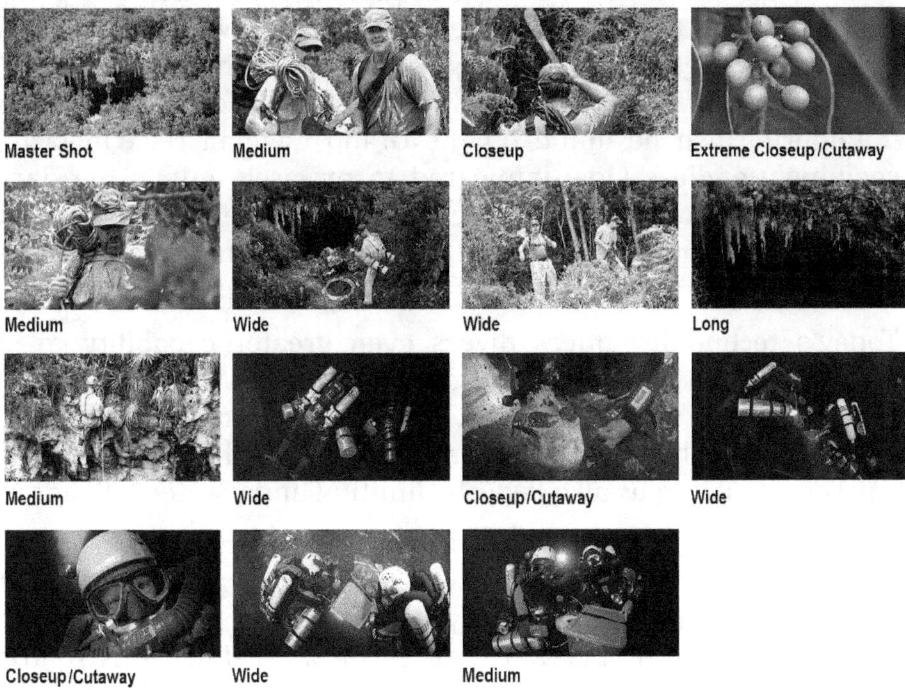

If you want to see the whole story about Extreme Cave Diving, watch the movie here for free: http://www.pbs.org/wgbh/nova/earth/extreme-cave-diving.html

Shooting Dive Vacation Videos

When I was a young diver I recall being invited over to my neighbor Danny's house to watch his first underwater vacation video. It was shot on a nifty High-8 camera in an oversized Ikelite housing. To this day, I have no idea how he got that massive thing to the Cayman Islands and back on a commercial airplane.

Our rag-tag group of Toronto aquanauts, armed with cold six-packs and warm pizza, descended to his sunken living room and crowded onto a large, garishly green velour sectional couch. Eager to see stingrays and sharks captured by our brave, budding underwater cameraman, we anxiously anticipated a production on par with the Undersea World of Jacques Cousteau. The inviting, saturated tropical colors would refresh our dull eyes, dogged by a long grey Canadian winter.

An hour into the tape, I was certain that his production was going to be longer than the vacation itself. Worse yet, I was feeling seasick. Danny had captured every single moment of his dives, including every jerky inflation of his BCD, every mask clearing and every floundering fish he found on the Grand Cayman reef. In fact, his seemingly endless video appeared to precisely mimic the darting motion of his over enthusiastic eyeballs. While the ethereal Enya soundtrack droned on, I dug out some Dramamine from my bag and opened another beer. How many tapes could he have possibly shot?

Today's technology offers divers even greater capability to stuff hours of HD footage onto tiny memory cards. Worse yet, with the proliferation of mobile devices, they can upload it to the Internet and instantly share it with friends! In my ideal world, Vimeo and YouTube could do us all a favor by limiting underwater uploads to 3-5 minutes.

So, how do you make an underwater video that people will want to watch? There are a few things you can study that will make you a better filmmaker. But beware; once you start down this road you may never be able to watch film and television in the same way again.

Deconstructing the Edit

If you watch television, you will notice that the story is constructed of lots of relatively short shots that represent different points of view. These small clips are lumped together in editing to tell a cohesive story. Using brief vignettes, the story is constructed in a way that accelerates time. Just because your dive took forty minutes to complete, does not mean the film should be 40 minutes long. The goal is to create a reel of highlights that tells a narrative that feels complete.

A successful short underwater video might open with a ten-second "master shot" of the boat leaving the dock with people waving. The next shot could show a series of close-ups of people assembling gear; a regulator being pressurized, an SPG showing a full tank, a quick smile from a dive buddy or a dive flag in the breeze. Next, you might insert a water-level-view of a diver jumping off the boat, followed by a team descending the line. In this short 30-second open, you have already established the boat, the divers, and the activity.

People are Important

You might feel like your vacation was all about your first encounter with a whale shark, but that will only hold a viewer's attention for a brief period of time. Ultimately, stories need to have characters, and those won't be just the type with dorsal fins. Your vacation video should include people. The viewer needs to be able to relate to the joy of diving and should feel like they could be a part of the adventure themselves. Chasing fish butts around the reef won't be too exciting, but witnessing a diver swimming beside a fish while removing his regulator and grinning will make the audience smile too.

Edit with Motion

Look for short shots that include some type of motion. If a fish turns and swims from left to right in the frame, the follow up shot could show a diver looking up or swimming right to left to give the illusion that they are swimming towards the fish. Move your camera slowly and deliberately to tilt up or pan across a reef. Reveal subjects by tilting up or down to them and then slowly track with the motion of the subject. All your motion should be intentional and slow. Frenetic camera movements will only make your audience nauseous. Helmet mounted GoPro cameras are the worst. The small camera exaggerates fast movements.

Don't Edit in the Camera

Your final edit will be constructed of short shots, so when you capture footage be sure to count to five after the action has passed. If you are shooting a passing manta ray, keep the camera rolling for five seconds after it leaves the frame. This editing "handle" will be important for allowing transitions, such as cross-dissolves, in the edit. You should leave a five second handle on the beginning of a shot too. Many new shooters are already thinking about the next shot and clip their footage far too tight. By leaving long tails at the beginning and end of a clip, you will gain versatility and creative freedom in the editing process.

Keep it Short

Your first vacation video should be under five minutes in total run-time; preferably under three. When you begin your project with a time in mind, you'll be more disciplined to find the very best of your footage and construct a tight and engaging story. Its better to leave your audience begging for more than dreading your next invitation for a post-trip video party. You get the beer, and I'll bring the pizza!

Here is a video example describing a trip to Christmas Island: https://vimeo.com/77177009

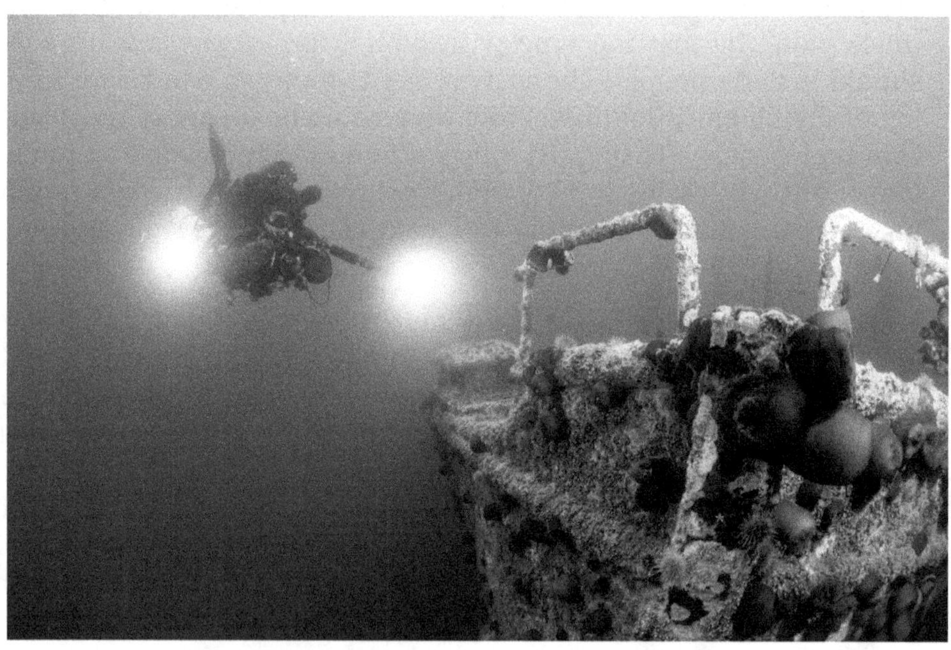

Cas Dobbin shots the bow of a WWII shipwreck in Newfoundland. Photo: Jill Heinerth

Camera Types

Shooting from Your Pocket

Micro HD Cameras Can Pack a Punch

With a degree in Visual Communications Design in hand, in 1988 I graduated from Toronto's York University and set out into the world to find a way to combine my creative talents with my love for the underwater world. Looking back over the past quarter century, I realize that the biggest advancement in capturing images of our underwater world is accessibility. These days, almost everyone has an opportunity to be a photographer or filmmaker. Equipped with inexpensive pocket-sized cameras that outperform the monster housings I used to lug through the water just a decade ago, capturing underwater video is no longer rare; it's routine. Armed with new technology, enthusiasm, and a little education, today's divers are able to gain a creative edge that separates their work from the lackluster shots of fish butts disappearing into the murk of a local quarry. Understanding the capabilities of your camera and capitalizing on those assets offers even an entry-level diver opportunities that were simply not afforded to us even a few years ago.

Until recently, I had to make a tough choice each time I jumped in the water. Would I shoot video or stills? I had to own, maintain and prepare two separate systems and then make a difficult decision; bring back video of manta rays dancing in the light, or try to capture the iconic still shot of the menacing leviathan, mouth agape and swimming towards the camera. Fortunately there are many cameras that can do both now and fortunately some of those cameras are also inexpensive. Micro HD camera systems popularized by companies such as GoPro are palm-sized wonders. You can do everything in one dive; shoot a video piece, switch to stills and even produce a time-lapse interval segment that has remarkable resolution at an economical price.

So, just what is HD?

To begin, we should first look at what constitutes a high definition camera and how we can tell the differences. The distinction between older formats, lumped into the category of Standard Definition (SD) and High Definition (HD), is primarily the resolution. In video formats that we are familiar with viewing on televisions or computers, the resolution is defined by the number of horizontal lines of information that make up the picture. SD footage generally contains 480 lines of information, where HD footage contains up to 1080 lines of material. The more lines of information that make up a picture, the sharper the video will appear. Most HD video cameras today offer either 720 or 1080 lines of resolution and are additionally described with either an "i" or a "p," which indicates either "interlaced" or "progressive" scanned frames. You may see 720i or 1080p on the spec sheet.

With a progressive scanned video, such as "1080p," the camera records each line of information from the top to the bottom of the frame. Progressive scanning lends a "film-like" look that is similar to what we see in movie theaters.

Recording interlaced footage, such as "720i," the camera skips every second line but moves through the frames at twice the speed. In the first frame, the camera records lines 1, 3, 5, 7, etc. and the following frame records 2, 4, 6, 8 and so on. The human eye is able to assemble these alternating frames into a cohesive picture that has a very immediate look, such as we see in most television news footage.

Today, HD cameras are available in a wide choice of price ranges - from $200 to $200,000 USD. Significant differences between these cameras lie in the quantity of data that is recorded, the lenses available, quality and size of the sensor, and how much the data is compressed. Although a 720p model may be referred to as an HD camera, the term "Full HD" is generally reserved for cameras that offer at least 1920 x 1080 resolution. A camera that records a lot of data will have a high "bit rate," which is described in megabits per second (Mbps). The more data you are recording, the better the image. And, the less you are compressing it, the better the data.

In a nutshell, if you are evaluating two different cameras that record Full HD at a resolution of 1920 x 1080, then you should look at the bit rate to determine which is likely to offer a better picture. Higher bit rates will look better. Beyond that, a myriad of features dictate the price, and generally, the quality of the end product and the versatility of manual controls.

Micro HD cameras such as the GoPro HD Hero series and similar pocket action cameras represent entry-level, yet highly capable hybrid cameras. For under $300, divers can equip themselves with a tiny, housed camera, with download cables, mounting hardware and everything they need to get wet. The GoPro system offers an optional viewfinder back and varying resolutions as the price range increases.

The HD Hero was originally designed for extreme sports enthusiasts such as surfers, snowboarders and BMX bikers, but scuba divers quickly realized this tool had terrific potential in recreational diving depths. When they were first released, underwater users reported fuzzy looking footage, so after-market engineers responded, creating flat-port underwater housings that could correct for focus errors. With these upgraded housings from manufacturers such as Eye of Mine, Backscatter and Sartek, the vignetting (darkened corners) and soft focus was eliminated. Now, a truly powerful underwater camera was born. Golem Gear jumped in the game with a remarkable deep housing, capable of staggering depths for technical divers.

Several challenges still exist with shooting these Micro HD hybrids. Holding a tiny camera in a stable manner is difficult and if you move it around too much, you'll risk making your audience seasick before the first act. Secondly, they require significant additional light to achieve the highest quality images of the twilight depths and color-filtered world of a reef, wreck or cave.

To combat these stability challenges, GoPro cameras come packaged with a series of helmet, wrist and other mounts that can be used to stabilize footage. An entire industry of other products from camera trays, control arms and lighting has also found their way into the underwater marketplace from manufacturers including Light and Motion, Backscatter and others.

Micro HD cameras shoot in auto exposure and auto focus modes. That means that you can't control the exposure with camera controls. It's actually a great way to learn to shoot, because it forces you to look at the available light and figure out how to get the best shot. These cameras take a little time to adjust to exposure changes, so it is wise to "lock off" a shot and hold the camera stable for a nice long sequence. Beginner videographers often get wrapped up in the experience and bounce around too quickly between takes. Once you have selected a scene, hold the camera still for five-seconds before and after your shot to ensure you have recorded the "moment" with sufficient handles for editing. Avoid the harshest, high contrasts of full light to full blackness. The camera will do a much better job of capturing the shot in more subtle, mid contrast range lighting scenarios.

Backscatter has manufactured a unique housing with glass flat port and a filter holder that offers additional control over challenging exposure scenarios, such as half-in, half-out shots. (Part of the lens is underwater while the other half is on the surface.) Installing a graduated neutral density (ND) filter can recover an overexposed sky and various colored filters or gradients can offer interesting creative effects for stills, video or time lapse. Their "Magic Filter" is terrific for shallow shooting without additional lighting.

In a nutshell, here are my four key tips to becoming a better underwater shooter with Micro HD:

1. Avoid fast jerky movements and record a long segment to allow for exposure and focus capture as well as adequate editing handles.

2. Use a flat-port housing that eliminates vignette and offers tack sharp focus.

3. Consider adding an after market camera tray for stabilization and the ability to carry video lights.

4. Use desiccant strips inside your housing if water temperature causes lens fogging.

Great GoPro Hacks

GoPros are becoming ubiquitous in the dive world. These little devices are awesome for traveling light and capturing great underwater moments. Yet unavoidable issues sometimes get in the way of bringing home the best possible footage. Here are four of the best tips for correcting and recovering your sport camera's footage.

How to Recover a Flooded GoPro

Some people say that everyone will eventually flood an underwater camera. Most of the time water and electronics don't mix, but GoPro cameras are surprisingly resilient if the emergency is handled quickly and effectively.

If you see bubbles coming out of the housing or see water sloshing around in the housing, safely exit the water as quickly as possible.

Remove battery and memory card from the camera immediately and set them aside.

Rinse the camera and card in clean, filtered tap water. (If water is not filtered, then mineral residue may disrupt contacts).

Discard the battery in an environmentally responsible way.

Shake out excess water.

Dry the camera with a towel while being careful not to scratch the lens.

Place camera inside a Ziploc© bag, partially filled with dry white rice. (The rice will act as a desiccant, helping to wick up moisture).

Allow time to fully dry. This can be achieved in several ways: in a sunny car for one day, in air conditioned room for two days, in room temperature for up to two weeks, or use a hair dryer or vacuum cleaner to cheat a bit, and assist in faster dry times (turn off the heat).

Buy a fresh battery.

If you use a battery back, install your fresh battery in the backpack and press the button to test. The green lights will illuminate if it is okay. Test the backpack on the camera. If you don't use a battery backpack, then reinstall the card and battery and test the camera.

If your camera was flooded in fresh water there is a good chance this process will restore the camera to its former glory. If it was flooded in salt water, it still may work as long as the battery was removed quickly and the camera was rinsed immediately. Salt water flooding is, obviously, a more serious event than fresh.

If you are not having success recovering your camera following these steps, then additionally, try cleaning any electrical contacts on the camera and battery with a product such as DeOxIt Gold.

Be sure to test the housing for leaks (without installing the camera) before taking your camera on your next dive.

How to Correct Blue Footage

You can correct for the blue tint of water by using a special red filter made by numerous manufacturers. You can also upgrade to a better filter system such as the Red Flip Filter from Backscatter.

This filter has a series of different colors that can be flipped into position based on your depth.

If you already have the footage "in the can" you can color correct using your favorite editing program. GoPro offers the CineForm editing plug-in as a free download from their website. Other programs such as FinalCutX or Abode Premiere offer even more features.

There are a few simple steps you can employ using editing software to make your footage look more like the way you intended when you captured it:

1. Use a sharpening filter.

2. In the white balance tool, move the slider slowly from blue towards yellow until it looks right to your eye. You are warming up the image by lowering the color temperature.

3. Slide the tint tool from green towards red/magenta.

4. Look at the highlights in your image to ensure you have not gone too far and tinted them pink. Continue to adjust each slider until it looks right.

5. Increase the contrast.

6. Shift the exposure slider to brighten up the shot.

7. Review the entire shot sequence to ensure that your corrections appear consistent throughout the entire range of light in the shot.

8. Work in short clips for color correction. Attempting to correct a long sequence might take significant system memory and time.

How to Steady Your Shots

There is nothing worse than watching GoPro footage shot from a helmet or mask mount. On first consideration, it might seem like a great idea, but the reality is that we move our heads around too much to create stable footage. Your viewers will get seasick watching your clips. There are several ways to steady your footage:

1. Breathe deep and swim slowly.

2. Pan the camera very slowly with deliberate moves.

3. Use a tray with built in handles and lights such as this Light and Motion's kit.

4. Use an extension pole such as the GoPole Evo floating extension pole to film forward or make whole-body selfie footage. If you drop it, you won't lose your camera as long as you follow it to the surface!

5. Use optical stabilizing features in editing programs that smooth out some jerky movements.

How to Remove Water Spots from the Lens

It's really fun to shoot at water level when your buddy leaps off the boat. It's also fun to shoot in the rain, on the waterside and in the sprinkler system. But, water spots can really ruin your footage. If you are shooting at water level, it is unlikely that you can dry your camera with a towel and ask for a reshoot. The easiest way to quickly clean the lens and start over is to lick it a couple of times. This is also a self-test to see if you are a serious videographer! (Yes. With your tongue! Saliva on your fingers won't work quite as well.) It removes spots effectively and sheds the water on subsequent takes. When you download your footage later, you'll have a good laugh looking at all your crazy tongue shots!

The GoPro camera has revolutionized underwater video shooting by putting small and capable devices in almost everyone's dive bag. There is no telling where this technology will take us next, but in the interim, these small tips will improve your footage and help you recover your video masterpiece from a bad day out.

iPhone Video

Deep within a Central Florida storm sewer network, I slogged through the greasy runoff of busy highways and overcrowded parking lots. Even for a seasoned expedition diver like me, this was a unique assignment - scouting the dark bowels of an urban cave network for a documentary film about fresh water issues. The grungy water cascaded over the edges of slippery concrete chutes, and splashed down into side channels and branching conduits. The black water disappeared down oily conduits, draining poisons from a matrix of asphalt ribbons above me. It was slippery and smelled like an oil refinery. Losing my footing, I hunched over to stop myself from falling, and in painful slow motion, I watched my new iPhone slip out of my chest pocket and splash into the grimy soup at my feet. Can you hear me now?

Smelling like a garbage truck, I climbed a rusty set of rungs to a heavy manhole and heaved my way into a parking lot of a busy strip mall. Crawling out of the breach in the pavement, my luck was improving. There was an AT&T store across the plaza. I must have shocked the young salesman, and, certain that he wanted to dispatch this odoriferous mad woman from his store, he replaced my phone in a matter of minutes. Mere months later, I lost a second phone to moisture, this time caused by the dangerous perils of a cup holder full of the sweet stickiness of my Diet Coke.

Today, we carry our lives in our smart phones and the thought of losing one to water damage is nightmarish. So why would anyone choose to risk their precious iPhone in the unforgiving depths of scuba dive? Underwater video. The video capturing quality of the modern iPhone is quite remarkable, and the convenience and size for travel is unmatched.

The iPhone 5s may be getting outdated, but a recent search on the web saw them selling on eBay and elsewhere for between $50 and $100. That's pretty decent considering the built-in ability to shoot 1080p HD video recording (30 fps) with slo-mo video capability at 120 fps and video stabilization. Now there's no reason to risk your invaluable iPhone when you can get a cheap backup for water time. If you are willing to expand your wallet and get an iPhone 6, then the stakes are raised considerably. Upgraded an even better CMOS Digital Imaging Sensor, it continual autofocus and cinematic video stabilization. Improved image stabilization enhances the liquid glory of a moving dive sequence. If rumors are true, then the next generation of iPhones will jump even further ahead of their competitors.

There have always been inexpensive "sealed bag" options for iPhone water protection and flimsy cases for talking in the rain, but now there are professional alternatives for serious divers who want to shoot with Apple's amazing and versatile little smartphone.

Most recently, a product called LenzO was released for the iPhone6. It appears to be the most advanced underwater housing for the smart phone market, containing color correction filters, access to native app camera modes, an optically correct dome and optional diopter, sunshade, Bluetooth trigger and other features. The best news is that manufacturer Vals Tech has announced the release of the device for other smartphone models: iPhone 6 Plus, Samsung Note, Galaxy S6, S6 Edge.

The Lenzo Smart Phone Housing from Vals Tech

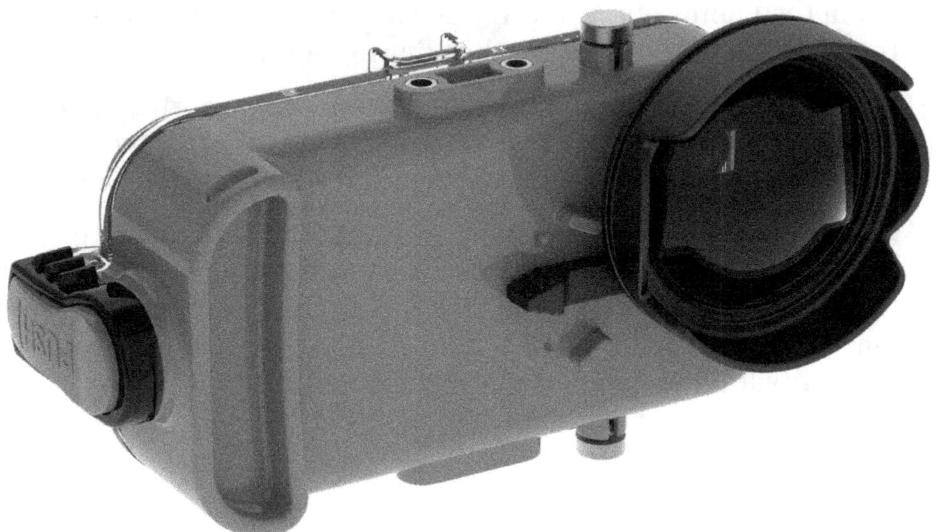

How to Shoot with your Smart Phone

Whether you choose to use the professional-level case or something else on the market, there are a few key tips to remember when shooting video with an iPhone. The underwater world is glorious tableau of colorful moving subjects. Hold your camera still and allow the image to be recorded in its own continuous motion. There is no need for quick movements that distract the viewer and challenge the camera's capability. The iPhone offers a convenient continual autofocus and auto-exposure feature that functions well underwater as long as you keep your shots relatively stable. Slow pans from side to side are effective if you maintain a consistent distance from your subject. Fast moving objects are sometimes too quick for the camera as it samples to catch up. Tilt-up and tilt-down camera moves must be extremely slow to allow the camera to make exposure and focus changes without the appearance of "stepped ratcheting." Close-up targets reveal the best color saturation and rich detail. As with any camera, the more distant you are from the subject, the more washed out your image will be.

iPhone Editing

You can trim a video on an iPhone or iPad using the included Photos app. This will help you throw away extraneous footage that uses up precious space. You'll able to drag anchors form the right and left to shorten your clip. You can trim the original or save a new shorter clip.

Within the Photos app you can also share or send your video to others or publish to YouTube or other sharing services.

If you want to do something beyond trimming a short clip, you can also edit right on your iPhone with iMovie or other software. Video apps will let you filter, adjust, stabilize and add transitions and titles.

Whether you plan on snorkeling in the Caribbean, diving on deep walls or boldly navigating the perils of your car's cup holder, there are finally viable options for protecting your iPhone from water damage. As the capability of iPhone's onboard camera features improve, it will be tougher to resist the simplicity of traveling with a serious pocket-sized filmmaking tool.

Point and Shoot Video

There are many compact cameras on the market, but there are fewer that are optimized for underwater shooting. With new camera models emerging faster than sharks to a chum ball, there is normally a lag between new camera releases and the availability of a housing to take them underwater. Manufacturers have to hedge their bets and forecast the best sale's potential then invest in engineering to get it wet. As such, the cameras we use underwater may not be the newest and best featured models on the market.

Regardless of the video system you select, there are several considerations to keep in mind. Specifications can be difficult to compare and a primer on some features is helpful. Specialist sites such as Backscatter and Reef Photo offer reviews and updates on new technology. Online forums such as WetPixel provide a podium for third party reviews by individuals.

Get Close

As with any camera is critically important to get as close to your subject as possible, especially if your visibility conditions are limited. Every inch of water between you and your subject, filters color and light. Keeping that in mind, a wide-angle lens offers the best chance to get close and still get a wide angle of view. Many shooters steer towards ultra-wide and fisheye lenses to increase clarity and color, but that choice also comes with fisheye distortion. Marine life shots are more forgiving of fisheye distortion than portraits. Vertical lines in wrecks become distorted in a fisheye lens, but many photographers like the intimacy of getting close.

Choosing a camera with an optical zoom capability will offer more latitude in shooting, but if given the choice, always swim closer to a subject rather than zooming through filtering water.

Control Options

Point and shoot cameras always have an automatic mode for exposure, white balance and other features. The more additional controls that are available, the more money you are likely to spend. Having option such as ISO control, manual exposure controls and relatively common, but higher resolution video format choices and zebra controls are really useful if you can afford a camera with those features. Companies such as Sea and Sea manufacture "all-in-one" kits for new videographers, but it is also possible to get a housing made for almost any camera on the market. Ikelite will custom build a housing to your specifications.

Video Lighting for Compacts

Flashes and strobes are used for still photographs, but a videographer may need additional lighting to reveal the vibrant colors of a reef or diver. If you want to escape the bonds of a monochromatic study in blue, you will need to add video lighting to your camera. Mounted on camera arms, these lights are the secret to color and clarity. A light that is angled towards the subject will produce the appearance of better visibility than one that hits the subject head on.

Video lights allow a shooter to work independently, but if you want the best results, you need to get the lights off the camera and into the hands of a lighting assistant. A system that can be detached from the camera will be far more versatile than one that is dependent on a camera mounted battery pack or arm system. Some primary lights used by cave and wreck divers can be retrofitted with a video reflector that spreads and softens the beam of light, helping it to illuminate a much wider area with diffused, even light but a tight beam primary light is ineffective and distracting – sort of like watching a cat chase a laser pointer around the room!

Low Light Sensitivity

The ISO specification for a camera demonstrates the light sensitivity of the camera sensor. Comparing shots from different camera models, shot in low light conditions will reveal that when digital cameras begin to struggle in the darkness, they usually create digital artifacts called color noise. Color noise appears as pixels of inappropriate color in areas that should be quite dark or black in a photograph. It makes a shot appear grainy and when editing corrections are attempted the results become garish and exaggerated. A camera that shoots well in low light conditions is very helpful in the often dark and muted underwater world.

Memory Capability

Most cameras are capable of shooting more than your wildest imagination can ever record on a given dive. Cameras generally ship with small memory cards and can be quickly upgraded by adding a faster, larger capacity card. Video shooters need cards that are "fast" in order to keep up with the stream of data that is being sent through the sensor. In the end, it is rarely the card size that limits the diver's ability to gather stills and video. Ordinarily, the battery or lighting system goes down before a card is fully utilized. It is important to offload your footage each day and reformat the card to allow for maximal use and to avoid potential card errors that could leave you without images form your favorite dive. That means you will either need multiple cards, a laptop or potentially even a hard drive to manage the data from shooting on a vacation. A GoPro download can quickly hog all your remaining disk space on your computer. Editing that footage will require even more space. The storage requirements can get quite large with the resolutions available today.

When is comes down to the finish line, price point is usually tied to features and capability. Housing manufacturers have already made the choice about which cameras offer the best features for divers. The amount of money you spend will be proportional to the features and capability of the camera system you end up with. If you want to upgrade, do it sooner than later. Camera systems are generally considered obsolete inside two years. Although they are still capable of shooting great images, their value on the open market decreases with every day beyond release.

Links for underwater camera retailers:

www.BandHPhotoVideo.com

www.Backscatter.com

www.ReefPhoto.com

www.Adorama.com

www.LeisurePro.com

Shooting with the Big Guns

HDSLR Cameras

High Definition Digital Single Lens Reflex (HDSLR) cameras are capable of shooting the highest quality stills while also delivering incredible uncompressed HD video capabilities. I have shot entire feature documentary films on a Canon 5D MK IIs. Without missing a beat, I was able to momentarily pause filming to shoot press kit still images and then switch back.

For me, the benefits of owning an HDSLR over a standard video camera are huge. Over the past few years, camera manufacturers such as Nikon and Canon were upgrading their high-end models faster than my budget could handle. Who knew that a two-year old professional still camera system could become obsolete so quickly? Not so with the latest crop of HDSLR's. My Canon 5D system allows me to keep using my expensive lenses, dome ports, viewfinders and accessories and, when necessary, replace only the camera body and housing without losing my entire investment. But the primary benefit to me, an underwater shooter who travels frequently, is having the dual capability of stills and video in a small package that fits in carryon baggage.

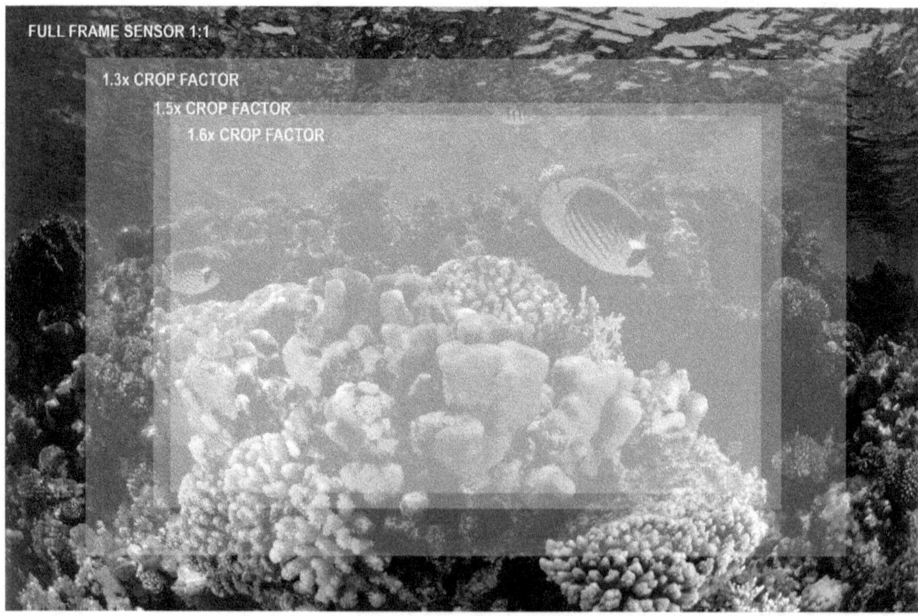

When navigating the scores of HDSLR choices, you'll likely be challenged with interpreting new jargon and discover a wide array of prices. One of the main factors that can affect price and performance is something called "crop factor" or "sensor format."

The sensor size of digital cameras is compared to the physical dimensions of the film plane of a 35mm SLR, and is used to describe the relative quality of the final image. A "full frame" sensor designates a camera that captures image quality that is equivalent to a 35mm SLR film camera. In an effort to reduce cost and weight, most HDSLRs are built with sensors that are smaller than a 35mm SLR's film plane. When you take a photo with these sensors, a smaller light sensitive area will be used compared to one with a larger sensor.

"Crop factor" or "sensor format" will also affect how your lenses operate on HDSLR cameras. Some lenses are built specifically for particular sensor formats, but traditional full frame, or standard lenses, act differently on small sensor cameras. In a nutshell, a wide-angle lens will not appear as wide as it would if placed on a full frame sensor camera, but a long lens provides increased magnification. This won't be much help underwater, but it is a bonus for people who like shooting distant subjects such as birds.

Equivalent Lens Sizes for Various Crop Factors

If you buy a 10mm lens, it will appear cropped on another camera. On a 1.3x cropped sensor, it will look like a 13mm lens. On a smaller 1.5x cropped sensor, it will appear like a 15mm lens.

Film Speed and ISO

Most digital camera features have their roots in 35mm SLR film cameras. Another "holdover term" from SLRs is ISO capability or sensitivity. This is commonly referred to as film speed.

These numbers are used to indicate the sensitivity of a certain type of film stock. "ISO" is the acronym for International Standards Organization. This independent testing organization created light sensitivity standards for photographic film that helped us to determine equivalency between different brands. A low ISO number like 25 indicates a "slow" film or one that requires more light to make an acceptable exposure. ISO 25 film stock is a good choice for macro work where detail and color are important and lots of light can be directed on the subject. A high ISO film like 1600 is extremely sensitive to light and is a good choice when using faster shutter speeds to capture action.

Traditional film stock contained a light sensitive emulsion known as silver halide. The larger the size of each grain of silver, the more sensitive it was to light. As the image was enlarged, the grain became more visible. Higher ISO film produced "grainy" results. Lower ISO's created finer grained images. Even though we now use a sensor instead of film, the same rules apply. A low ISO value will net the richest, most saturated color with the least amount of grain, but requires more light. The only difference now is that we refer to the relative graininess of the data from digital sensors as "noise" instead of "grain."

The reason why this is important to you as a potential purchaser is that a high ISO sensitivity will offer you much better capability in low light situations. Most diving scenarios are considered to be low light environments and a camera with a high sensor ISO capability will offer you many more clear shooting opportunities with minimized noise.

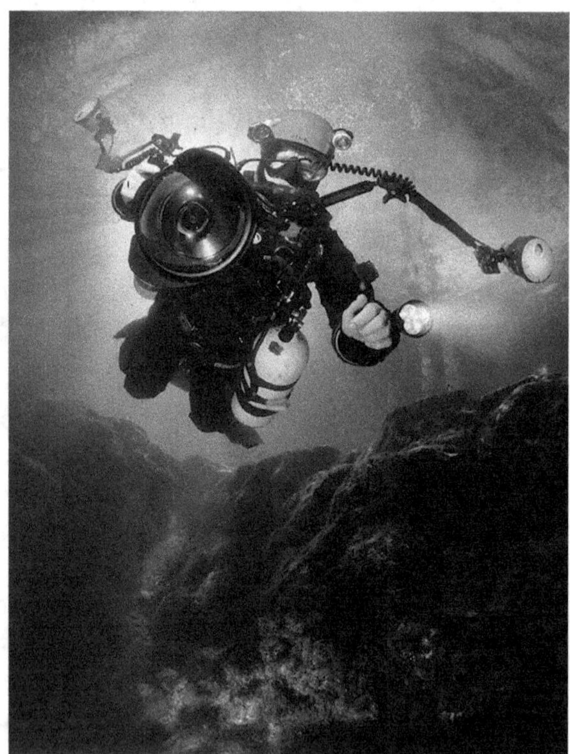

The author shooting a Canon HDSLR in an Aquatica housing. The camera is capable of shooting stills and HD video. Photo by Becky Kagan Schott

Sensor Cleaning

Many SLR cameras feature an automatic sensor cleaning function that removes dust from the image sensor inside the camera. Sensor dust may be prevented by waiting five-seconds after turning off the camera, prior to changing lenses. The sensor plate is energized when the camera is on. It holds a charge of static electricity that sucks dust into the camera body when it is on and open. If allowed to rest for several seconds, the static will be discharged before the camera body is breached for lens changes. Never leave the camera body open in dusty conditions or in salt spray. You might never salvage the sensor from such an assault.

In the event that your sensor develops a dirt spot, this can either be removed in editing or the sensor may be carefully hand cleaned. Sensor swabbing is a delicate process. It must be done with the correct materials or the camera can be ruined. Many online retailers sell sensor swab kits with proper instructions for cleaning. Follow your camera manufacturer's guidelines if you have the need to manually clean the image sensor! Some manufacturers and repair facilities offer annual cleaning and repair services if you feel uncomfortable about doing this yourself. Ensure that you seek out a reputable firm to take on this delicate task.

Watch this trailer to see footage shot on the Canon 5d mkiis in the Aquatica housing: https://vimeo.com/77177009

Micro Four Thirds Format

Micro Four Thirds Cameras look like baby DSLR cameras. They are small and lighter but still offer the flexibility of interchangeable lenses. Many of these cameras can use precisely the same lenses as their DSLR siblings with the support of an adapter ring. The crop factor of this camera is 1.3x, but unlike a DSLR, it does not rely on a mirror and prism to display the image through the viewfinder. The display is provided digitally on an LCD back and also through the digital viewfinder. This means the camera is considerably lighter and smaller. The capabilities of these cameras are growing faster, especially in their video features. Many are capable of excellent 4K ultra HD shooting at a fraction of the cost of a DSLR. They may not offer the same capability in shooting stills, but the video quality and professional level features generally surpass most DSLR cameras.

Check out this footage shot using the Panasonic GH4 micro four-thirds mirrorless camera in an Aquatica housing. The footage was shot in 4k resolution and was compressed to HD: https://vimeo.com/116898167

The Purchasing Choice

Financing an underwater HDSLR or Micro Four Thirds Mirrorless camera system is a major investment. My husband's dual sport motorcycle was far less expensive than some of my camera systems. But, if you are interested in shooting professional-grade uncompressed HD video *and* high-resolution stills, there is no way around the cost. You'll have to become a wise consumer. Decide on whether you want a great still camera that also shoots video or one that features great video with the ability to shoot reasonable still photos too. Regardless of what you spend on an underwater system, it is creativity, lighting and an interesting story that will set you apart from the underwater crowd on YouTube. Great videos have been shot on iPhones and inexpensive cameras.

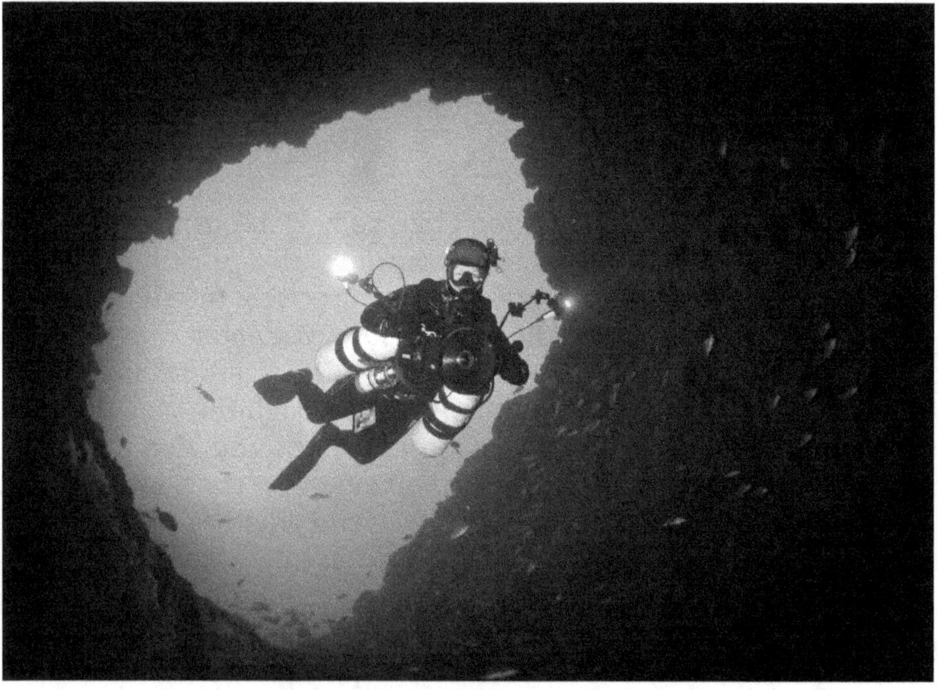

The author working on a project in Greater Exuma, Bahamas. Photo: Brian Kakuk

Lenses for Digital Cameras

Lenses are described by their focal length - fisheye, wide-angle, normal, and telephoto. Most underwater photographers seek out wide-angle lenses to couple with their digital SLR (DSLR) camera. Wide-angle lenses help the photographer to get close to the subject and minimize the amount of light- and color-filtering water between the camera and the subject. Telephoto lenses are not useful in the underwater environment because of reasons described above. It is not practical to take a long distance photo through light-filtering water that is often filled with particulate.

Fixed focal length lenses are known as prime lenses. Variable focal length lenses are referred to as zoom lenses. Lenses are also rated for speed, which is a numerical value based on the largest possible aperture, or iris opening. A "fast" lens is one that allows the photographer to select a smaller f-stop number like f/1.4. The lower the f-stop number, the larger the aperture opening. This can be confusing, but just remember that a small number represents a bigger opening, and a big number represents a smaller opening. An f-stop of f/1.4 allows more light to strike the image area than an f-stop of f/2.8. A slow lens will be rated with a higher f-stop number like f/4. The faster a lens is rated, the more functional it will be in lower light conditions. Divers should try to get as fast a lens as they can afford, since most underwater scenarios are light deprived. Another variable in selecting a lens is whether it can be automatically focused, or whether it only allows for manual focus operation. Finally, lenses are rated as professional when they are durably built, to meet the demands of changing environments, and with extremely high quality, polished glass elements.

Some DSLR and mirrorless cameras, such as some models of Nikon or Panasonic, use a digital sensor area that is smaller than the equivalent image area of 35 mm film. There are advantages and disadvantages to this feature, depending on what type of shooting you like to do. Older and standard Nikon lenses behave differently on film cameras than their digital counterparts. The sensor image area in some Nikon DSLR cameras is cropped by a factor of about 1.5 times. That means that a wildlife photographer who owns a standard 200 mm telephoto lens will find that it has the equivalent focal length of a 300 mm lens, when used with a crop sensor DSLR camera body. Standard SLR lens distances are significantly enhanced when coupled to a DSLR with a cropped sensor. On the other hand, people who love shooting wide-angle shots discover a narrower field of view when they put their old 17-35 mm on their new digital camera. This lens has the equivalent field of view of a 26-52 mm lens on a cropped sensor. Newer Nikon lenses labeled "DX" give true focal lengths (similar to those of a 35 mm SLR) based on the cropped sensor.

Full-frame sensor cameras offer a sensor image area that is equivalent in size to a 35 mm film stock. If you own DX or other cropped-sensor lenses, the image becomes cropped, but standard lenses operate to their full and best capacity.

Finally, an even more advanced type of lens is entering the arena. Manufacturers are now developing specialty lenses with enhanced optics that are matched to their cropped sensors and are designed for the unique requirements of the digital realm.

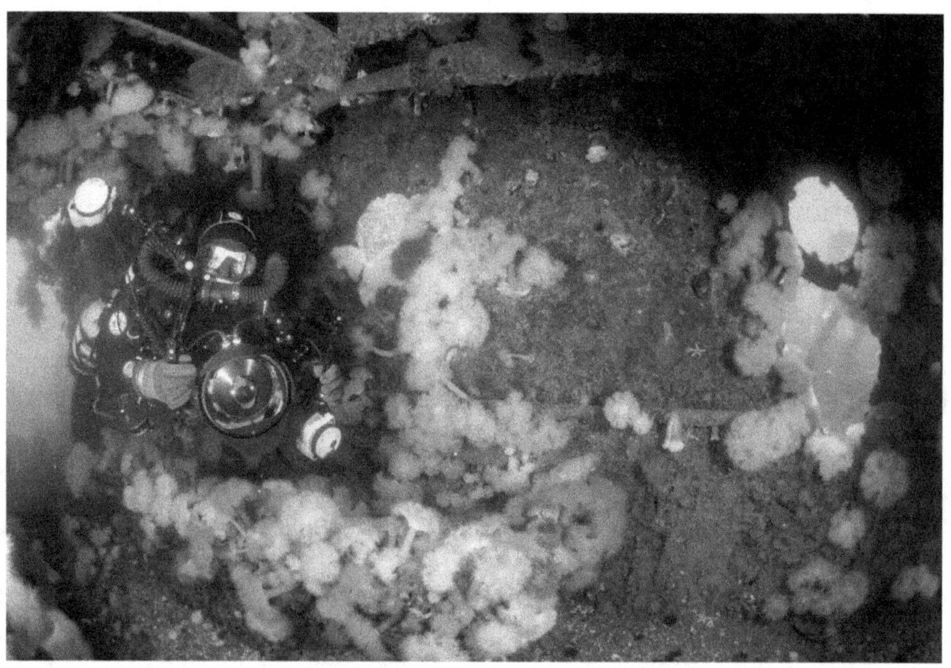

The author documenting WWII wrecks in Newfoundland. Photo: Cas Dobbin

What it takes to Shoot a Feature Film

Gliding along with the precise synchronicity of a flight demonstration team, scuba divers piloting radical-looking scooters maneuver into the frame. As viewers we are transformed, drawn into the dimly lit cave of indescribable beauty. If the Director of Photography (DP) has done his job, we are engrossed in the wonder of the story. Some people have said that feature films are like sausage. They might be tasty to consume, but you don't necessarily want to see how they are made. On the contrary, I am going to assume that the readers of this book are eager to know the nitty gritty details of what it takes to make a feature movie.

A few years ago, I got a call from a Hollywood studio asking me to lead the Underwater Unit in making the movie **The Cave**. Little did I know at the time, my daily role would include producing, stunt diving, directing, script supervision, wardrobe consultation and safety. I even had to help build the rebreathers used in the film, and train the actors to dive them. My job would defy description and cross over to every department on the set. With over 1500 people involved in making The Cave, that also meant a lot of new friends.

I spent almost eight months in Los Angeles and Romania in the prep and set shooting, but it was the location work in Mexico that was the most memorable. We had completed all the stunts, tricks and anything that might damage a cave environment within the confines of constructed caves on set, and were ready to move on to beauty shots in natural caves. It was a monumental task of organization, bringing 40 people together in the jungle for one month to get the job done.

The underwater footage in Mexico was shot using a Sony F900-3 camera in an Amphibico housing. While Unit Director Garry Phillips could sit inside an air-conditioned tent with an HD engineer and audio specialist, Wes Skiles, myself, and 16 other cave divers were hard at work bringing the scenes to life underwater. This meant that an incredibly long cable was needed to connect Phillips to Skiles deep inside a cenote within Sistema Dos Ojos. Every inch of that cable had to be managed by a team of divers to ensure that we did no damage to the pristine cave.

I recall one particular dive with great clarity. After an entire morning of preparation and rehearsal, Brian Kakuk and I were dressed appropriately in the wardrobe of the actors for whom we were doubling. I was playing Fast and Furious star Cole Hauser, grandson of media magnate Jack Warner (Warner Brothers) and Brian was on deck as Morris Chestnut, of Anaconda fame. My job was to drive a scooter while pulling a large sled filled with about 600 pounds of weighted Pelican cases and packs while Brian hung on and steered from behind. A squadron of divers delicately threaded their way into a gallery of stunning cave formations. Tom Morris and Woody Jasper slipped behind some large speleothems carrying huge lights, deftly maneuvering them to avoid disturbing the silt. Other underwater grips quickly followed their lead. Mark Long eased the slate in front of the camera and hit the clapper while Wes pulled his final white balance. Safety divers held with Brian and I at the launch point behind the camera.

"Speed... and ACTION!" Wes hollered through his Ocean Systems comms. My ear bud crackled with the indication to launch and I hit the throttle on full.

We glided over Wes as close as we could to create an illusion similar to the Millennium Falcon soaring through space. I heard him voice "yeahhhh." Panning our lights around the cave in a well-orchestrated dance, Wes commanded, "Uncover one. Uncover two. Uncover three. Cover one. Cover two. Uncover four." One at a time, the underwater grips sprang into action. With each order, a large garbage can lid was eased off of a lighting fixture, revealing the light briefly before slowly hiding it as we drove beyond the mark. Each diver was either hidden out of frame or concealed by their rebreather, prohibited from creating any bubbles that would destroy the illusion.

"And... CUT!" Wes yelled. I heard Garry's voice from topside declare, "wow!" Then my heart sank when I realized my scooter was stuck and would not turn off. We had been struggling with sticky triggers throughout the shoot, but here I was in this remarkable museum of crystalline formations, unable to stop.

Frantically, I yelled to Brian, "let go! I can't stop this thing," while darting between rocks and running away from our colleagues. I didn't want to horse collar him on an overhang and was hoping he might be able to jettison the 10-foot sled from my crotch strap. But my brother in cave diving had other ideas, "I'm staying with you he screamed back." And so we went on a wild ride, dodging stalagmites and weaving through silty corridors determined not to make any damage. I pounded on the magnetic read switch and then on the housing of the scooter. Having experienced the sticky switch before, I now carried a two-pound chunk of lead in my glove for just such an emergency. Swinging my arm like a circus strongman with a sledgehammer, it didn't make a bit of difference. Brian hung on yelling, "woo hoo!" and laughing at our predicament, while safety divers hopelessly gave up the chase. Wes, wondering where the talent had disappeared to, rallied the team out of the cave.

Finally many spine-chilling minutes down the road, Brian and I lapped back to the entrance and finished our joy ride. I found a spot by the deck to bury the nose of the scooter into the silt and detached myself from the bucking underwater bronco. A topside team manhandled the runaway scooter from the water, opened the housing, and detached the battery. Injury averted. Wildly spinning prop blades neutralized. This experience is one of the many reasons I think that cave diving for movies is even more dangerous than the real thing!

In the end, the critics panned The Cave. However, there was huge kudos for the impressive underwater scenes. Unfortunately, the stunning beauty of The Cave could not overcome the clichés and weak character building of the plot.

If you are looking to pass an evening enjoying extraordinary underwater videography, and can ignore a bit of sensational Hollywood drama, then check out The Cave.

I'm the diver girl, playing all the diver guys...

Dedicated Video Cameras

It appears that we have reached the point in technology where dedicated video-only cameras are going the way of the dinosaur – at least for consumer divers. Professional camera operators still tote behemoths with names like Red, Dragon, EPIC and Scarlett. These pro cameras can handle everything from 8K to 3D, ultra high speed to IMAX sized projection. Suffice to say, an entire book can be written and re-written almost monthly on the developments in the broadcast industry. We'll consider that beyond the scope of this book.

As a dive enthusiast rather than professional broadcast cinematographer, you still might find a great deal on an older dedicated video camera. Tape-based formats are rapidly disappearing, but if you can find a memory card based camera, it still might be worthwhile to pick up. The key consideration for tape-based cameras is to confirm that your camera will jive with your editing equipment. Check the connections on the camera and your laptop and confirm that your editing program can ingest the footage that you are capturing on the camera. Remember that you will need the camera (or a dedicated deck) to download footage to your computer. That means you need to keep the camera even if you upgrade to a better model later; otherwise your tape library will be caught in limbo… great footage, but no way to get it on to a computer.

Professional broadcast cameras and consumer/prosumer models are also converging in the underwater world. 6K footage might offer incredible potential topside, but as soon as you take a professional 6K camera into marginal visibility, you are dealing with conditions that will erase some of the greatest benefits of resolution. If the visibility is 40 feet with "chunky" water then it might as well be a soft veil over a great camera. Professional cameras like the RED series may also require significant color grading end editing before you can display decent looking footage. The material is recorded in a RAW format that required plenty of processing. That may be more than you are willing to deal with or more than your editing computer can ingest and edit.

The Dive

Camera Prep and Testing

Follow these steps to prepare for your dive:

1. Before you do anything else, check to ensure that you have a freshly formatted, empty memory card in your camera. Check that your battery life is adequate to get through your dive day and recharge if necessary. Carefully clean the camera lens using lens tissue or a specialized lens cloth. Never use towels or clothing to clean a camera lens as it may become irreparably scratched. If there is a stubborn stain or grease on the lens, place a couple of drops of lens cleaner on a lens tissue and then rub the lens. Do not drop cleaning fluid directly on the camera lens.

2. Carefully inspect the camera housing and dome port for damage and dirt. The interior of the housing must be free of dirt, hair and grease that can end up in front of the lens. Canned air or even a scuba tank with a low-pressure nozzle may be used to carefully remove dirt from the interior of a housing.

3. Thoroughly inspect and clean all O-Rings according to the manufacturer's instructions. They should never be removed with anything sharp, since they can be easily damaged.

4. Use a small amount of silicone lubricant to put a slight sheen on O-Rings. Never use excessive amounts since that may cause leakage.

5. Place the camera in the housing according to the manufacturer's directions. Follow instructions carefully. The camera should not be difficult to install in the housing if all the buttons are in the correct position. Incorrect assembly can result in damaged buttons and levers or eventual leakage. Use a vacuum pump to pressure test if applicable.

6. Assemble the light arms according to the manufacturer's instructions and angle the lights toward the subject.

7. Turn on the camera and briefly test the lights. Test the focus and other buttons for proper function. Fire a test shot to ensure functionality of the strobe units or slaves.

8. Place the camera in a rinse bucket to test for leaks before diving, or carefully place the camera in the water if entering from shore. If

the housing has a leak detector, ensure the camera is powered on and listen for the beep or look for the leak detector light to ensure everything is fine. Bubbles escaping from any part of the system, means that water is getting in to your housing. If so, remove immediately and hold the housing in a way that lessens the likelihood of water touching the camera itself.

9. If you are entering the water by giant stride or back roll, have someone pass the camera down to you in the water. Jumping or rolling into the water with a camera may result in immediate, catastrophic flooding.

Getting in the Water

After the camera has been passed to you in the water, check all functions and look for bubbles. As you descend, check the dome port for small micro bubbles and gently rub them off to clear the lens. Be careful of rings or jewelry that could scratch the dome!

Exiting the Water

When you are ready to leave your safety stop, check the housing carefully for anything that does not appear to be seated properly like battery doors, lens ports or cable fittings. Anything loose will stay in place at fifteen feet, but as pressure is reduced and surface conditions bounce the diver and housing around, the greatest risk of flooding occurs.

As soon as possible, pass the camera to topside personnel, carefully showing them what part of the housing they may safely grab. Ask them to gently place the camera on deck so that you can put it in the rinse tank yourself and guard against dome port scratches.

Changeovers

If you need to switch memory cards or batteries before your next dive, care should be taken to dry the camera as much as possible. Ensure your body is dry enough that you do not drip water into an open housing or camera. Pull down your exposure suit to your waist and put a towel on your head to prevent such mishaps.

When opening a housing or light on a boat or near water, plan to open the housing in a direction that will protect the interior from dripping water. Allow the water to run down and off of the housing. Use a towel to drape over yourself and the camera so that spray from divers and waves do not get into the system. Ensure the camera is turned off. With dry hands, carefully replace the batteries and/or card and immediately close the housing, watching carefully for pinched O-Rings. Safeguard used cards in a small waterproof case. Make sure you can identify which cards are used and which ones are fresh.

Follow the prep and test procedures, described previously, to ensure that all elements of the camera are still properly aligned in the housing.

Post Dive Care

Immediately after a saltwater dive, you can use a spray bottle of Salt-X to prevent encrustation of minerals on the housing. As soon as possible, soak the camera housing in freshwater and depress all the buttons to guarantee thorough rinsing and to get all the salt out of the controls.

Freshwater dives and pool sessions may also necessitate immediate washing of your camera housing. The dome port of the housing may develop hazing or mineral spots if left un-rinsed. These deposits may be impossible to remove if allowed to dry fully.

Mineral deposits are like wet concrete. They are very easy to rinse and remove when wet and almost impossible to wash away after they have set.

Did You Know? – Explosive Damage

Did you know that a camera housing that is closed up tight in airline baggage could explode? It doesn't exactly blow to pieces, but a button or port may fail and breach the waterproof integrity of the unit. Camera housings are designed for positive pressure and may not withstand negative pressure.

Always travel with a door open or O-Rings removed.

The 80 lb. Parka

Airline baggage limitations are getting more stringent every day. There was a time when I could fly on a media pass and take unlimited extras for $25 a piece, up to 100 pounds. I recall one instance where I flew from LA to Washington, London and Bucharest with 28 pieces and a $3500 bill for extra baggage. Now, extra baggage is nearly impossible.

A few years back, I flew to Ekaterinberg, Russia, at a time when baggage embargoes were strict. I needed to travel to the edge of Siberia with a video package, photo gear, cave diving equipment and something to keep me warm for a couple of weeks. The biggest challenge was the weight limitation. I was allowed two; fifty-pound bags and a single carry on. This was clearly going to be impossible, so I took the heaviest batteries and regulators and lenses and loaded them in my wheeled carry-on case. I could hardly lift it onto the inspection conveyor. But, as the airlines had no "wear-it-on" limitations, I decided to pack as much dive and camera gear as humanly possible into the pockets, nooks and crannies of my Antarctic parka. I wore several layers of clothing and my heavy winter boots as I embarked on the plane in balmy Florida. Once safely seated, I began to strip down layers and deposited them in a folding shopping bag I had stuffed in a pocket. On arrival in London, I donned the bulky layers again, heaved my heavy parka laden with goodies over my shoulders and shuffled through international security.

As I approached the X-ray, I began removing all the layers and boots and placed them in the plastic bins. Laptop in one. Boots in another. Parka overflowing. Six bins later, I walked through the metal detector and got patted down for looking so heavily stuffed.

Beyond the X-ray I had to empty every pocket of the 80 lb. parka and explain my way through security. Rather than being annoyed, the affable British officers were easily amused by my persistence and strength.

As I struggled down the aisle on my Moscow connection, I was relieved to discover that my carryon actually fit in the overhead bin. The 40-kilogram limit obviously exceeded by my single bag, I took a risk and heaved the overloaded parka into the tray and settled into my seat for the next leg of travel. Its no wonder flying is so tiring. It's a workout.

Pre-Dive Checklist

Most of us agree that good diving procedures help keep divers safe. Following protocols can also safeguard your camera gear, while increasing the likelihood that you will return with great shots. If you follow these steps each time you plan a video dive, you'll protect your investment, while bringing home memorable underwater video assets.

Pack with Care: It may not be possible to carry your camera and housing in carry-on baggage. Luggage weight limits are increasingly constraining, and sturdy Pelican style cases are simply too heavy. An alternative to consider is placing a plastic bin such as a Rubbermaid© tote inside your large dive pack or duffle bag. Carefully pack your components in the bin with proper air filled or Styrofoam packing materials. Resist the urge to simply wrap sensitive gear in your wetsuit. When airline inspectors pull the wetsuit out of the bag, your camera may fly across the room. If you wrap with foam or bubble wrap, tape and label each item and consider placing a letter or packing slip that describes all items in the top of the luggage. Bring extra tape for the trip home. You may also want to take a photo of your gear sitting on the tote before it is packed. Print the photo, and place it on top of everything inside the tote. The objective is to make it as easy as possible for inspectors to understand what you have wrapped inside your bag.

Set Yourself Up for Success: Assemble your camera and housing and seal it in a cool, dry, well-lit area. This will minimize the moisture inside the housing and reduce the likelihood that you will trap something like a desiccant pack in the housing door. Assembly on a hot humid boat may lead to condensation or fogging. If your housing is equipped with a vacuum pump, check the seal and always carry extra batteries for the leak detector. Double check any locking latches or port locks to ensure they are secure.

Test All Functions: After preparing your camera, test the record function. Verify the camera settings including the ISO and quality setting. Verify that the camera will focus. Ensure all critical knobs and buttons are fully functioning. If you fail to check these things, there will come a day when you get underwater and discover the lens cap is still on or the ON/OFF control is jammed.

Be Patient: If you discover that something is not working, take your time to fix the problem and start your preparation from the beginning again. Many floods occur when someone hastily opens a housing to flip a switch or re-position a lever. Inspect everything carefully, reseal the housing, and recheck all functions before submerging.

Pre Set for Descent: Dial in the camera settings that you think will be useful for descent. Make sure the camera is on and ready to shoot in case you have a remarkable underwater encounter right at the beginning of the dive. Sometimes it is being in the right place at the right time, prepared to capture the unexpected events, that leads to award-winning shots!

Be Gentle to Your Camera: Always have your rig handed to you by the surface crew, while you are already in the water. Never jump in with your camera in hand. The most likely place for a flood is on the surface when things can easily be dislodged. If there are no personnel available to pass you a camera, then hang your camera off your own gear line and retrieve it when you descend.

Bring Your Own Bucket: Think twice before using the boat's rinse bucket. There are many hazards floating in their bucket. Divers who rinse their mask in the camera bucket may be contaminating it with defog and other chemicals as well as sunscreen from their hands. When your camera bounces around with others in the common bin, it is also likely to get damaged. The port can get scratched or the housing flooded as the boat lurches in the waves. Bring your own collapsible cooler or plastic bin (like the one described in packing above). If fresh water is not available, then bring a wet towel to protect your camera between dives. A lightweight camping towel will take up very little space in your luggage. A product such as Salt-X can be sprayed on the housing to prevent salts from drying and sticking tot he housing.

Protect from the Sun: In order to prevent fogging, never let your underwater housing sit in the sun either before or between dives. Drape a wet towel over the camera housing. Compact cameras and Go-Pros are the most susceptible to fogging, so don't leave them lying in the sun on the deck.

Train the Crew: When you exit the water, train the crew to replace your dome port covers as soon as possible to avoid scratches. Even a minor blemish on a GoPro lens can look like the Grand Canyon in your shot. Let the crew know precisely where you want your camera placed until you are able to attend to it. Don't let them put it on a bench where it might fall. Avoid the boat rinse bucket and attend to your gear yourself as soon as you have removed your own equipment.

Be Prepared: Bring the necessary items onboard to take care of yourself. This kit can include: your own bucket or collapsible cooler, a wet towel to drape over the camera, a dry towel in case you need to open the housing, a second dry towel for your head in case you need to open the housing and want to prevent dripping in to the housing, a vacuum pump to open/close the housing, screwdrivers or Allen keys to tighten ball mounts and handles, Salt-X, port cover, lens cleaning tissue, O-ring lube, spare parts, spare batteries for the camera and leak detector, and spare memory cards in a waterproof card wallet.

You may want to consider printing a checklist, laminating it, and carrying it in your gear bag. Even after decades of professional underwater shooting, I refer to checklists I have created for each piece of gear I carry. Treat your camera as highly valuable equipment, and, with each dive, you will bring back priceless underwater video treasure.

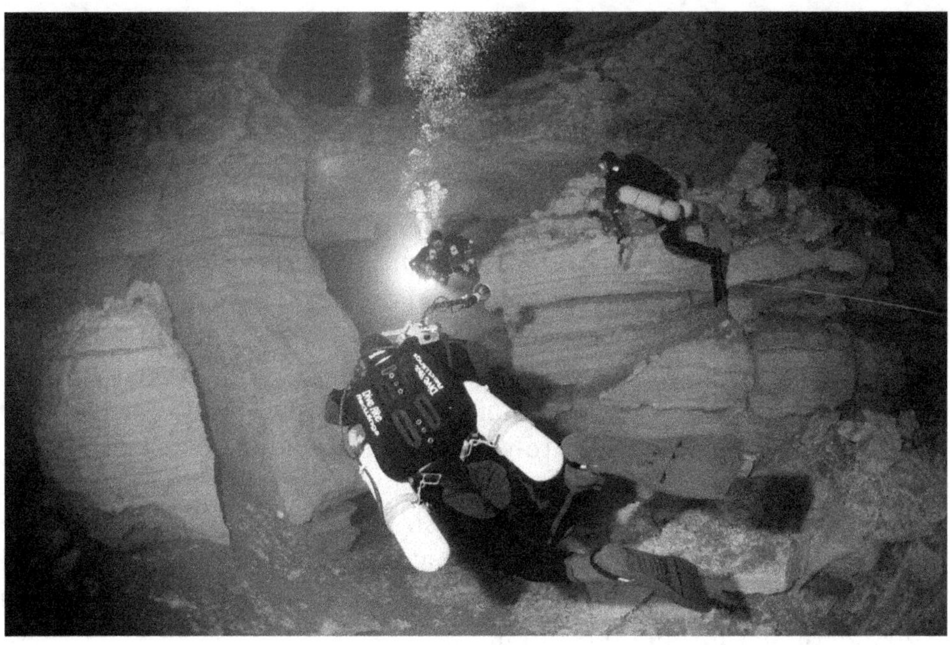

Dive team filming in Ordinskaya Cave in Russia. Photo: Jill Heinerth

Exposure Control

My old Nikonos V underwater camera had a big green "A" on the dial. Most people never moved that dial off of the "A" position except to switch it to the familiar red "R" that allowed you to rewind the film safely back into its lightproof metal canister. It is hard to believe that I gave up that camera only a decade ago. Well, "gave up" is a generous term. All of my prized underwater camera gear was stolen on the night of the wrap party, after a long gig on the Hollywood movie "The Cave." We were all on the beach drowning in tequila while the (so-called) security guard for our lodging invited all his friends to divest our rooms of all our valuables.

As a result, I was reluctantly torn from my love affair with film emulsion and thrust into digital cameras in 2005. My new Nikon DSLR had a familiar "A" on the dial, but I had been long warned against using that setting. An early Nikonos V mentor told me that, "A" stood for "Average" and not "Automatic" as I had understood. She clearly coached, "if you want to be truly creative you have to be smarter than the camera." Howard Hall, (another unknowing mentor) offered his best exposure advice, "f8 and be there!" I knew the wisdom resided somewhere in-between. My new camera had single-letter settings for Program, Aperture-Priority, Shutter-Priority and Manual. Clearly I was going to need to dig out my university notes and refresh myself in the theory of exposure if I wanted to be smarter than this camera.

In the earliest days of image making, photographers used a device called a "pinhole camera." This was simply a small box containing a roll or plate of light sensitive material or film. A tiny hole in the front of the box could be opened to allow light to strike the surface of the material. Larger holes allowed more light in, and produced a brighter exposure. When the hole was held open for a long duration, it gave time for more light to strike the film plane. The actual image exposure was a relationship of light intensity and time. The intensity of the light was controlled by the size of the pinhole and the time was controlled by the duration that the shutter curtain was held open. This relationship is expressed with an equation that forms the pivotal theory for all image making:

E = I x T which refers to **Exposure = Intensity x Time**

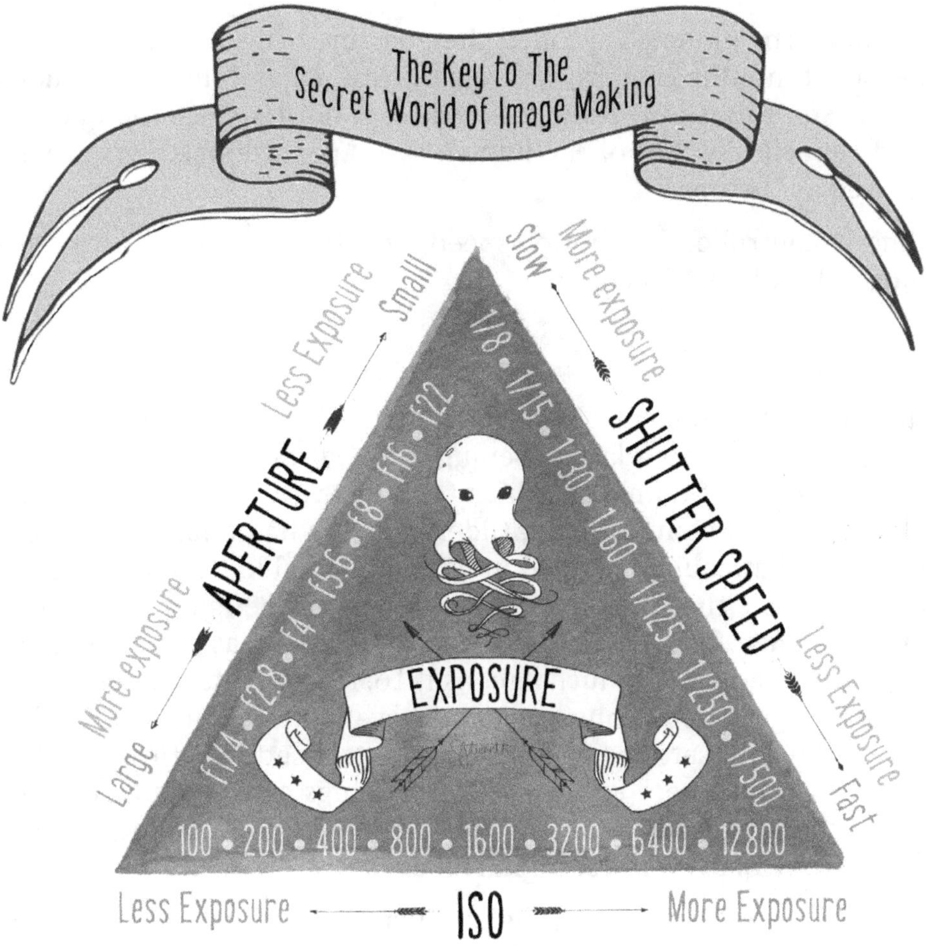

The Key to The Secret World of Image Making

Small
Less Exposure
APERTURE
More exposure
Large

f1/4 • f2.8 • f4 • f5.6 • f8 • f16 • f22

Slow
More exposure
SHUTTER SPEED
Less Exposure
Fast

1/8 • 1/15 • 1/30 • 1/60 • 1/125 • 1/250 • 1/500

EXPOSURE

100 • 200 • 400 • 800 • 1600 • 3200 • 6400 • 12800

Less Exposure ← ISO → More Exposure

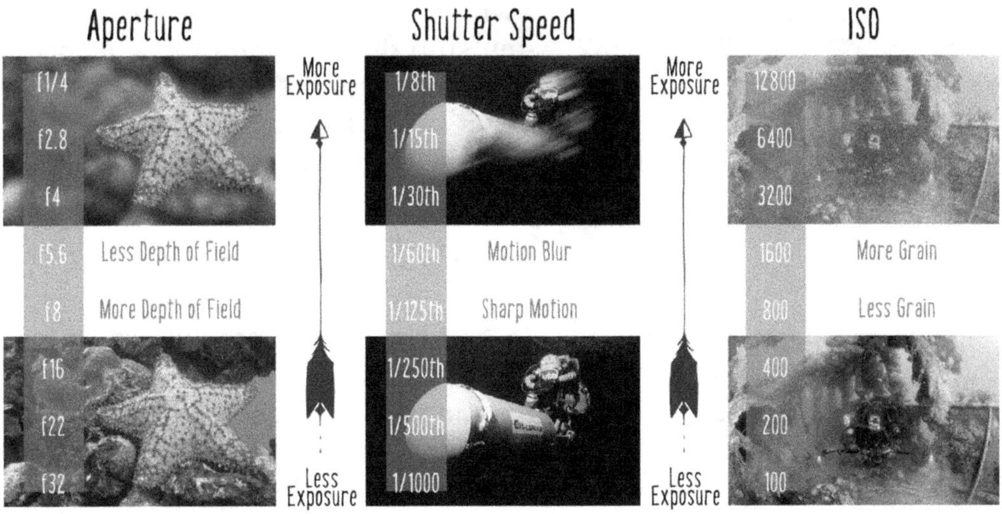

The modern "pinhole" is called the aperture. This opening, that allows light into the camera, controls the intensity of the light striking the sensor. It has also been referred to as an iris since the opening works much like that of the human eye. Aperture openings are expressed as "f-stops."

Time is controlled by shutter speed, which can be selected in seconds or fractions of seconds.

Aperture

Apertures or f-stops are expressed in sizes. A small f-stop number like f/2.8 represents a large opening, allowing access to high intensity light. A large f-number such as f/22 is a very small opening that admits a tiny amount of light. Older cameras had a limited number of f-stops that could be dialed in with a manual knob. Each stepped opening was either half or double the amount of light as the previous stop. Therefore, f/2.8 was twice as much light as f/5.6. Similarly, f/22 permitted half as much light as f/16. Many digital cameras have almost infinite selections of f-stops available when using either Manual Control settings or Aperture Control settings. However, like most modern camera controls, these settings are derived from historical cameras. Understanding this history helps the photographer master control over newer digital models.

When you buy a lens, one of the product specifications describes the limits of the aperture. A lens that can open up to a large aperture of f/2.8, f/1.8 or even larger is known as a "fast lens." Most lens will all close down to f/22 or f/32. A full stop difference on the specifications will indicate that the lens may be capable of requiring only half the light to illuminate a photo. That's why fast lenses are generally more expensive and usually a good selection for low light conditions like underwater video.

Controlling Time

Shutter Speed is expressed in increments of seconds such as 1/125th of a second, 1/500th of a second or 1 second. Light strikes the film or image sensor for this duration. In general, fast shutter speeds like 1/500, 1/1000 and higher will "freeze" the action making footage look crisp and immediate. Slow shutter speeds blur action, but they also allow maximum light penetration in dark environments.

ISO

ISO is one of three factors in the exposure equation for your still or video camera. ISO refers to the International Standards Organization, which determined a common specification for the sensitivity of manufactured acetate film stock emulsions. In film shooting, a high ISO film emulsion such as 1600 is highly sensitive to light, making it a good choice to capture the inside of an underwater wreck or cave. But tighter macro close-ups could benefit from lower ISO sensitivity. Commonly available films such as 100 ISO were generally developed for bright, sunny conditions. The relative graininess of the film and finished prints increased directly with higher ISO numbers. Today, ISO number refers not to the emulsion, but to the relative sensitivity of the camera sensor. The ISO settings typically start at 100 and continue to double from this point to the limit of your camera's capability: 100, 200, 400, 800, 1600, 3200, 64,000, etc. Some cameras offer unlimited stops in between these values.

Many new shooters disregard shutter speed, aperture and ISO controls on their camera and select an Automatic or Program setting that makes choices for them. However, understanding ISO will help you achieve precisely the results you desire and help you find a camera that will perform well within the latitudes of lighting you experience underwater.

In digital shooting, shutter speed determines how long the camera sensor will be exposed to light while aperture determines the size of the opening in the iris of the lens. ISO describes the relative sensitivity of the sensor plate itself. When shooting video, you can only lower the shutter speed to a point where the human eye is unable to piece together the series of still images into a smoothly rolling shot. Generally, below 30 frames per second (fps) we can start to see the slow motion and shuttered effect. At 15 fps, the slow motion effect is really obvious and the sequence appears very truncated. Therefore, if the shutter speed is as low as it can go and the iris is letting in as much light as possible (with a low f-stop number), then the only other control available is to crank the ISO number higher to make the sensor more sensitive. The downside is that the increased ISO number comes with more digital "noise" which is also called "gain" or "grain."

To understand how this works, you can think about your first stereo. As a young person with a fixation for entertaining your friends, you likely turned up the volume to blast out your best tunes. At some point you may have heard the audio quality degrading with crackles and feedback. When you turn up the volume or gain, you are amplifying a weak electronic signal to make it louder. That comes with a gradually distorted overall quality of sound. The same thing happens inside your camera. When you have a weak signal in a low light situation, you need to amplify the signal like turning up the volume. In doing so, you are increasing gain and getting more visual noise in your shot. There are some instances where this is unavoidable. You are better off getting a grainy shot of a distant eagle ray in the darkness than having no shot at all, but there are a few other things you can do to improve low light capability.

Larger sensors are generally more sensitive than small ones. That is why a large format camera shoots a better-looking sequence than a GoPro camera. That is also why some cameras can only produce standard definition, while others offer HD, 4K or even 8K streams. Larger sensors and more expensive cameras are priced based on available features, but also on the quality of the sensor itself. A faster lens will also help. Lenses are graded based on their largest f-stop. A lower f-number (smaller number, bigger iris opening) indicates a faster lens. Adding more light to a shot will boost your exposure lessening the need to crank the ISO up. GoPros can shoot amazing footage but they need a lot of external light when used in underwater environments.

Take control over your ISO setting by first planning the best exposure possible. Open up the aperture, lower the shutter speed and then select the lowest ISO speed the exposure will permit. If you were looking for an archival grainy film look, then add the effect in postproduction so you retain a clean master for other purposes. The good news is that a remarkable sequence will stand on its own merit. Strive for optimal exposure, but, if you have captured a magical underwater phenomenon, it will stand on its own, no matter how grainy the footage.

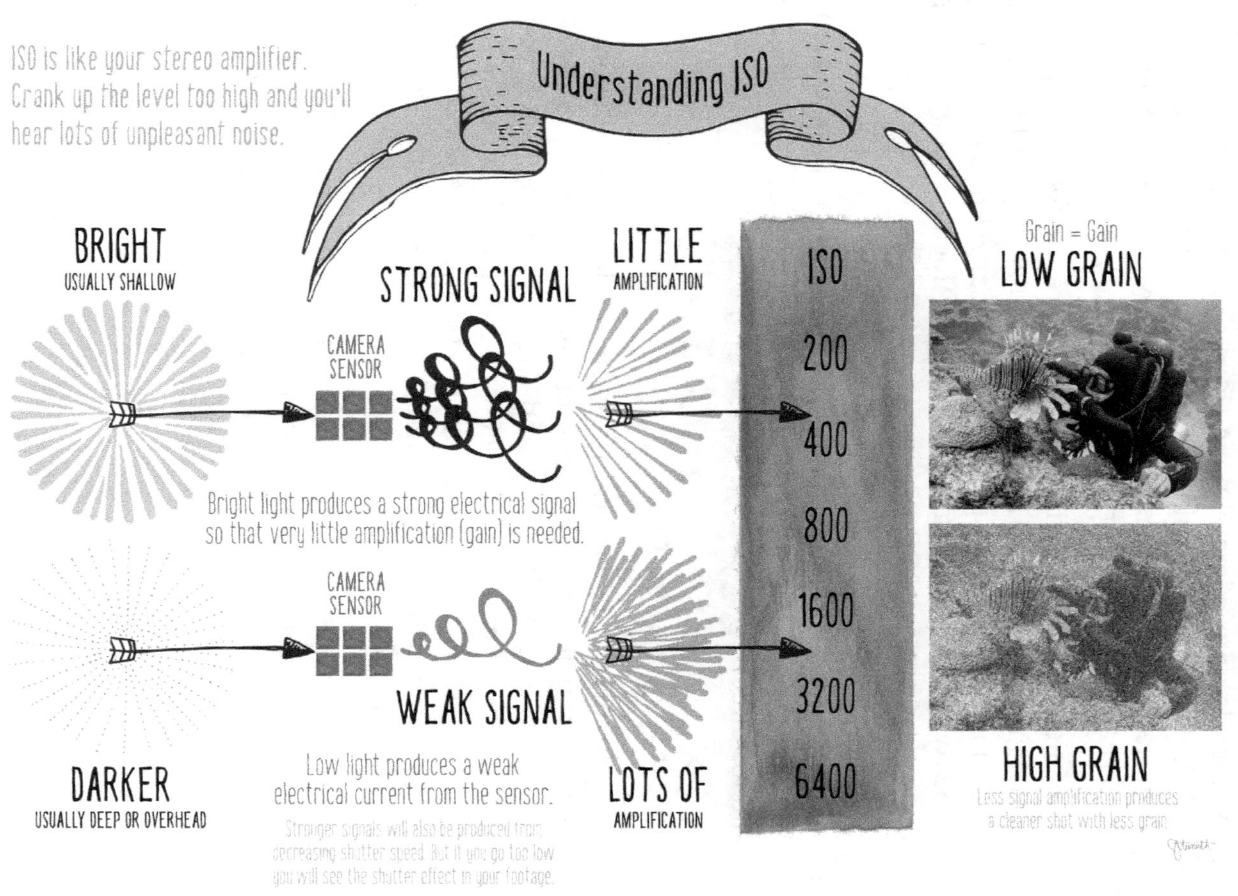
Understanding ISO
ISO is like your stereo amplifier.
Crank up the level too high and you'll
hear lots of unpleasant noise.
BRIGHT
USUALLY SHALLOW
CAMERA
SENSOR
STRONG SIGNAL
Bright light produces a strong electrical signal
so that very little amplification (gain) is needed.
LITTLE
AMPLIFICATION
DARKER
USUALLY DEEP OR OVERHEAD
CAMERA
SENSOR
WEAK SIGNAL
Low light produces a weak
electrical current from the sensor.
Stronger signals will also be produced from
decreasing shutter speed. But if you go too low
you will see the shutter effect in your footage.
LOTS OF
AMPLIFICATION
ISO
200
400
800
1600
3200
6400
Grain = Gain
LOW GRAIN
HIGH GRAIN
Less signal amplification produces
a cleaner shot with less grain

Depth of Field

Depth of Field is the zone of the shot that appears to be in sharp focus. It extends approximately one-third the distance in front of and two-thirds the distance behind the subject on which you are focused. Depth of field increases when you "stop-down" (use a smaller aperture) to create your exposure.

Depth of field is controlled by the aperture, or f-stop. Large apertures such as f/2.8, f/4 and f/5.6 will minimize depth of field or narrow the range of focus in a picture. Smaller apertures like f/16, f/22 and f/32 will allow for a greater range of focus or more depth of field.

Some cameras are also equipped with a feature called de-focus control. Essentially, this feature allows you to limit the depth of field of a shot. You can highlight a foreground subject and de-focus the background for effect.

Equivalent Exposure

Modern cameras have several programmable options beyond fully automatic control, yet many shooters never use these tools. Aperture Priority, Shutter Priority and Manual settings give you the chance to master control over the camera and obtain truly artistic results. Understanding how the camera thinks is the key to originality. You are smarter than your camera! Experiment with different settings to decide what you like.

Although equivalent exposures represent mathematically comparable amounts of light entering the camera, they will result in different looking photographs. One exposure may be optimal, but others may yield greater depth of field, special motion effects or the ability to stop action.

Many people carefully manage aperture settings to control depth of field in their photos. This is called Aperture Priority. With Aperture Priority, the photographer selects the desired f-stop and the camera will choose the best corresponding shutter speed. By selecting a small aperture like f/22, depth of field increases, but will require a longer shutter speed to achieve the best exposure. If you shoot a crowd of people at f/22, they may all be in focus. Yet, if you select a large aperture such as f/2.8, with a corresponding fast shutter speed, the depth of field decreases, and they may highlight one sharp person in a soft focus crowd.

The newest cameras offer preprogrammed selections like portrait, landscape, backlit or even night photography mode. Your camera manual will describe these settings fully, but be aware, these settings will usually apply unique depth of field effects. A portrait setting may offer a narrow depth of field, while landscape will offer greater. A night setting may open the aperture wide, sacrificing depth of field.

Understanding depth of field may be difficult at first, but if you experiment with different f-stops and pre-sets while shooting the same scene, it becomes very apparent.

Lighting

Beyond equipment, skill and safety issues, the water itself is a challenging medium for the photographer.

When sunlight hits the surface of the water, much of it is reflected back skyward. Very little light actually penetrates the surface to illuminate the depths. When the sun is almost directly overhead, the maximum amount of light penetrates the underwater environment. Many people prefer to take photographs between 10 am and 2 pm for this reason alone. At other times of day, sunlight strikes the surface of the water, reflecting back a greater majority of light. During these off hours, less light will penetrate, but it may reach your subject with a more intriguing angle and color. Pros often prefer shooting in the early morning and late-day light because the character of the light is much more compelling.

Shooting from below, in an upward direction, will separate the subject from the darker water of the depths.

Thinking About Light

Before you swim off into the interior of a wreck or a cave, you must first learn to shoot well in open water diving scenarios. Thinking about, and looking at light, is a critical aspect of every shot. The cavern zone or doorway of a wreck is one the prettiest places to film. Learn to see and appreciate what light is available and figure out how to control it. Take advantage of available light and then supplement with justified light (light that appears to come from a diver's hand-held light or from the sun penetrating through the water column).

A camera-mounted light is capable of filling the foreground areas with light, but you also need to plan the exposure so that the background light illuminates the rest of the shot. This is called balancing the exposure.

Imagine yourself in a completely dark room. When someone throws open the exterior door, it takes a moment for your eyes to adjust and see the green lawn outside the door. There is such a high contrast between the bright, outside light and environment that you are standing in, that it may be impossible to register the details of the interior of the door-frame, while still seeing the details of the green lawn. If someone turns on an interior light, both may appear better balanced.

As a videographer you can make creative choices. Do you want the silhouette of a black doorframe, with a beautiful green lawn? Do you want the details of the interior of the door with a glaring bright white light pouring in? Do you want to balance both? This is where the creativity starts.

An Introduction to Underwater Video Lights

Modern video lights come in several types based on differing bulb technologies. Halogen, High Intensity Discharge (HID) and Light Emitting Diode (LED) lights operate in different ways and each have unique properties. Halogen lights emit a warm glow on the red end of the spectrum, similar to a traditional incandescent lamp light bulb in your home. If you've ever seen old photographs shot with only lamplight, they appear to have a warm, orange-red quality. This effect is often mimicked by smart phone photography applications like Instagram. HID and LED lights offer illumination, which is much truer to the actual sunlight falling on a scene, and are balanced very similarly to daylight.

The greatest challenge for the video lighting consumer is to compare apples to apples. The nomenclature for lights is tricky and manufacturers often boast about wattage that does not translate to relative light intensity. When shopping for a bright light, you should compare "lumens," which is the measurement that quantifies the amount of visible light emitted form a source. The more lumens, the brighter the light. The pattern of light emitting from the head is also very important. If you shoot with a wide-angle lens, then you need a wide reflector on your video light. When comparing different lighting options, look at the pattern and spread of the beam. Some LED options which are made up of multiple bulbs, cast spotty, speckled light, whereas a single-bulb halogen or HID might create a more even cast. Traditional cave or wreck diving primary lights can rarely fulfill the task of video lighting because their beam pattern is simply too narrow. Some halogen and HID primary lights offer the ability of removing and replacing the reflector with a widely dispersed video reflector, but LED primary lights rarely offer this feature.

I personally own and frequently use all three flavors of lighting. HID lights are extremely bright and compact but the bulbs are fragile and expensive. The ballast in the light is the most costly component, and when flooded, is rarely salvageable. I had some custom halogen lights made for me by the great guys at Light Monkey so I could mix some beautiful warm light into my shots. Halogen light technology does not require a ballast and the bulbs are very cheap and easy to replace if broken. LED lights are changing faster than any other lighting technology, upgrading their power exponentially every season. The bulbs are long lasting and robust. The cutting edge of the LED's coming to market will soon allow divers to adjust the color temperature of lighting for any underwater scenario by activating a mixed array of red, green and blue LEDs.

In the end, your budget may have the biggest influence on your ultimate choice in lighting. In the next issue I will share tips and creative techniques so you can use your video lights like a pro!

Popular video light manufacturers:

www.LightandMotion.com

www.LightMonkey.us

www.Green-Force.com

Go to this link to see Light and Motion Sola lights and the Aquatica AGH4 housing with Panasonic GH4 mirrorless camera in action:

https://vimeo.com/131312935

Practical Lighting Techniques

Most underwater videographers buy a couple of lights and mount them to their camera on arms, illuminating the environment, or use a dive buddy to hold them at close range. Camera-mounted lights are generally acceptable for highlighting the main subjects in a scene, whether they are fish, fellow divers or a beautiful reef. However, if you want to elevate your creative underwater game, you may want to become familiar with "Practical Lighting Techniques." Practical light sources are defined as lighting sources that appear in a frame and can be perceived as a part of the on-screen world. In other words, they appear "justified." (Sometimes "justified light" and "practicals" are terms used as cinematic shorthand.) A handheld or helmet light on a diver would be considered practical lighting but so could a large light source, hidden from view that mimics the sun's rays cascading into the opening of a wreck. When topside, cinematographers paint a space with light using available lamps, windows, TV screens or streetlights to offer practical, justified light.

Often working in a cave or wreck, in a world of limited natural light, I use other divers to carry practical lights that bring depth and dimension to my underwater world. Yet, even on a bright day in shallow water, a practical light in a diver's hand can bring focus to your subject, and lead the viewer through a remarkable journey.

Types of Lighting

The video lights that are attached to your camera should offer a wide diffuse beam that casts soft light on a large field of view. These same lights can be used off camera to light up regions further away. Wide-angle lighting can fill extensive areas and also softly highlight the edges of divers and sea life. Held perpendicular to the camera lens, they sharpen edges helping subjects leap away from the background. The underwater world is a complicated and busy scene. When we sharpen layers of the scene or divide it into regions of light, then dimension and depth are enhanced.

There are numerous manufacturers of lights with wide beams. The price variation between lights may be found in size, lumens, burn time and the quality of build. Be sure to investigate the weight and general buoyancy characteristics of this type of lighting. If it will be hand carried by a diver, then it should be close to neutrally buoyant. A light that is negatively buoyant will not only fatigue your underwater model but it may also change their trim or exceed the lift capacity of their BCD.

Some practicals can be set stationary in a scene to enhance the illusion of sunlight accentuating a space. These instruments should be slightly negatively buoyant so they are stable in the current and surge. They can be mounted to small flexible tripods allowing them to be purposely directed. Care must be taken to avoid any environmental damage caused by placing a light in a scene. I have worked on Hollywood productions and television shows where the size of the practical lighting almost dwarfed the divers. These lights, cabled all the way to the surface for power, needed numerous divers to wrangle the light head and cord to protect the reef or cave.

Narrow beam lights also have an important place in practical lighting. A technical diver's canister light is more likely to be a narrow beam design. So are small handheld backup lights. These practicals act like light sabers, carrying the viewer's eyes around the scene. Instruct your model to "play" with the light, raking it around the scene, lighting up points of interest along the way. This movement adds power to a scene. If the diver is swimming directly towards the camera, caution them to point their light in a way that does not penetrate the lens for prolonged periods. It is okay and actually beautiful to periodically pass the light beam across the dome of the camera. This creates a momentary flare in the lens that can be effective. If the diver's eyes follow the light, we get the notion of exploration unfolding in the scene before us.

Use of Lights

Use practical lights in a variety of ways to diversify your underwater video. Models can either swim away from the camera or towards it using a searchlight technique. Divers can separate themselves from the background of a reef, wreck or cave by hiding a wide beamed light and directing it at the wall while you swim parallel with them, turning their body into more of a silhouette. Models can also be backlit by another diver. In this case, the first diver simply swims towards the camera while the diver behind them points their light directly at their partner's body in the direction of the camera. The diver's body acts as shield for the brightest center portion of the light and as a result, they are surrounded with a halo of light in the camera's point of view.

Practical lights add stimulation and purpose to movement through a frame. They can be of very minimal output, and still offer visual diversity that captures the viewer's interest. For examples of how to use interesting lighting techniques in your video, go to this link: https://vimeo.com/92673716

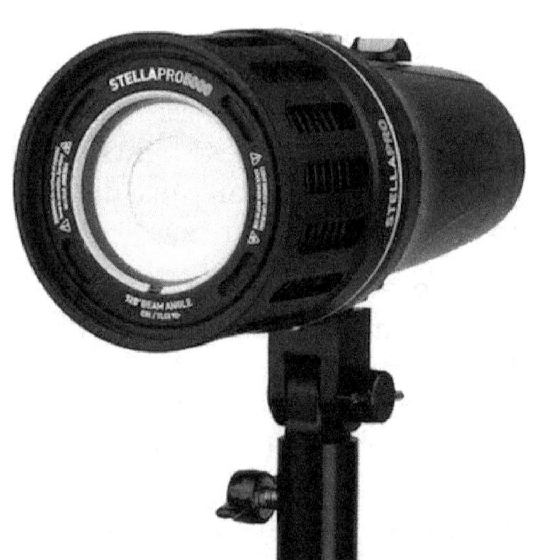

Multi purpose lights such as the Light and Motion Stella Pro series can be used topside as well as underwater. This can help keep travel gear light yet powerful.

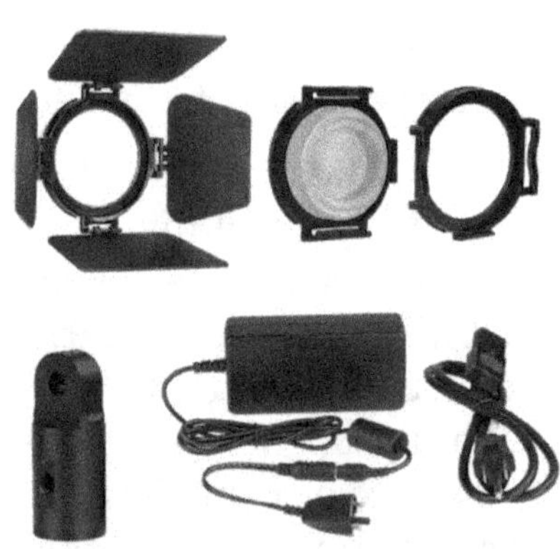

White Balance

If you are new to videography, white balance may be a new concept. White balance is a function on a digital camera that compensates for the different colorcasts that are emitted by various light sources. In simple terms – the reason we adjust white balance is to get the colors in your images as close to those of the original scene as possible. Underwater light sources may include sunlight, hand held diver's lights, or video lights. Water filters light in different ways, creating a wide variety of colors. Different depths alter natural light, and sometimes the results are less than pleasing. White balancing a camera compensates for those differences.

In the past, with film cameras, professionals would select film stock and filters based on lighting conditions. Indoor incandescent lighting called for "Tungsten" film, while basic outdoor photography was usually shot on "Daylight" balanced film. Selecting the proper film for the job would result in a nice, neutrally balanced photograph that approximated the original scene. Filters were also used to adjust different film types for the "color temperature" of the light. With digital cameras, we don't need to select different film or filters, but we do need to adjust white balance for the conditions of a given day, dive and even depth.

How Does White Balance Work?

When we "white balance" a camera, we teach the camera what white looks like on a particular day and condition. Once the camera makes white appear truly white, then every other color will look accurate under the same light sources. White balance can also be used to deliberately alter a color palette and introduce creative looks for special effects.

Digital cameras may have more than one technique for selecting white balance. Some cameras have an automatic feature that continuously re-samples for white balance. Some cameras allow the photographer to pre-program a variety of different white balances for different looks. High-end cameras will also allow the shooter to select a color temperature on the Kelvin temperature scale. To manually select white balance, the photographer carries a "white card" with them, so they always have a pure white reference. Entry-level cameras may not have a white balance control and may automatically self-calibrate white balance through the dive. In this case, unusual colorcasts may need to be corrected in post-processing.

Using a White Card

A white balance card can be clipped to a diver's equipment, but care should be taken to ensure that it does not drag and damage the fragile environment. To use a white balance card, place it in front of your lens so that white fills the field of view. If you are mixing a combination of different diving lights, ensure a little of each of those lights is spilling onto the card. You do not need to focus on the card, since you are only telling the camera to register the color white in the current water conditions. Ensure that some ambient light is spilling onto the card without casting shadows. You should not see any hot spots, glare or shadows on the card, but rather a soft mix of light. You might have to tilt the card to catch a little ambient light or zoom in close to fill the field of view.

Once the light looks even, depress the white balance button on your camera housing. Most cameras will take a few seconds to sample the light. While it is sampling you may see a flashing icon. Once the icon stops flashing, you will be able to see the new color shift through the viewfinder. If your white card has a color bar on it, you can reference that to see if it looks accurate. If things do not appear as desired, then try to white balance again.

If you are diving in bright and shallow conditions in open water, you might need to use the grey/blue side of the card to get an accurate color balance. Experiment with both sides of the card to see which gives you the best results. If you use a card that is not white, it will vary the colorcast of a photo. A light blue reference card will offer a warmer white balance that has a tinge of red. Professionals often use a light blue or 50% grey card to warm up flesh tones that tend to be overexposed underwater.

Aiming Video Lights

Videographers often have to overcome challenging visibility, but with good technique, you will bring home video that may look better than you recall from the dive itself. Video lights restore and saturate the natural color and illumination in a scene.

When divers invest in video lights, they generally purchase a matched pair of lights that can be affixed to their housing with flexible camera arms. Some lighting systems are proprietary to a particular housing manufacturer, while others may be adapted to fit different types of housings. I've had good results with Ultralight Control Systems. They manufacture a series of arms, fittings and adapters that allow divers to mix and match almost any system and affix it securely to a camera tray or housing.

Once your lights are secured to the housing, check the instruction manual to see whether it is okay to turn on the fixtures out of the water. If not, you may need to conduct your set up while submerged. Powerful video lights may become extremely hot when used topside. They can cause burns when touched and are hot enough to ignite a fire. They may also be damaged from the heat. Hot bulbs are fragile and handling with care is essential. Some HID bulbs may cost hundreds of dollars.

To aim your video lights, set up a target distance similar to the types of underwater subjects you will be shooting. Three feet is a good starting point. Aim the lights so that the beams just begin to overlap at the target distance. The area directly in front of your camera lens and the subject should be left in a cone of darkness. This way, silt and particulate that exist in the cone of darkness will not be illuminated, thus preventing backscatter. If you angle the lights too much and illuminate silt in front of the camera, then the silt and particulate will appear as large fuzzy spots in the footage. For this reason, wide-angle, soft beam video lights and reflectors offer the best flexibility. If you are shooting subjects that are farther away from your camera, you will need to angle the lighting fixtures even wider to increase the zone of darkness in front of the camera.

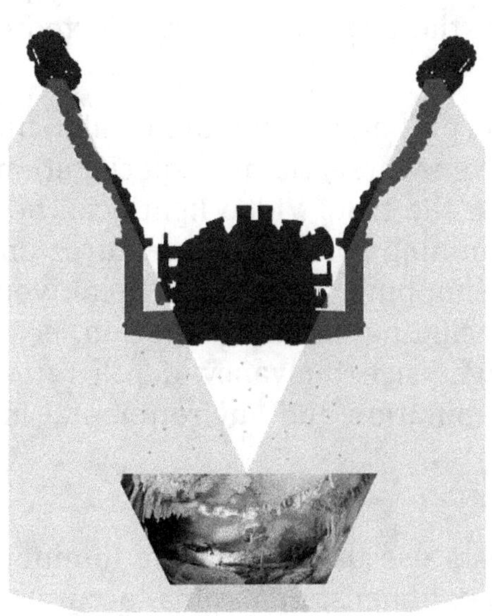

In order to minimize the effects of backscatter, angle your video lights so they illuminate the subject rather than the silty water between your camera and the subject.

If you are shooting macro shots of small animals that are very close to the camera, the lighting set up will be a little different. One light should be centered on the housing to shine down on the subject from above, while the second light may be angled from the side to provide fill light. The beams can be tighter since you are illuminating a smaller area.

It will take a few dives to get in the groove with your new lights. When you review your footage for backscatter and hot spots, it will help you shoot even better the next time.

How to Choose a Video Light

Let's begin with Jill's true confession: I have a bit of a light fetish. I can't seem to stop buying new lights. Headlamps, solar rechargeable, hand-cranked lanterns, cinema lighting, LED key fobs and endless cave diving and video lights. I have them all. And this doesn't include the numerous bicycle lights my husband Robert and I have collected, because, well, I can pin that one on him. Whew, I'm glad to finally share this and get it off my shoulders.

The fact is, lighting has improved exponentially since I began diving. In my early cave diving career, we lugged enormous sealed lead acid battery packs that powered feeble incandescent bulbs that barely lasted the duration of a single dive. If we had to carry those lights today, they would tip the scales at the airport and get rejected as hazardous cargo.

Light specifications are hard to interpret and even more challenging to compare from brand to brand. Even worse, claimed specifications rarely match actual performance in the field. Video lights can be a big investment, so it is worth examining some of the features and issues you should consider when shopping. You should break your research into several categories, including: lumens, duration, beam quality, coverage, burn curve, weight/size/buoyancy, depth rating, build quality, purpose, company reputation and environmental impact.

Lumens

The lumen is the unit that scientists use to examine the luminous flux from a light source. In essence, lumens, or lumina, accurately describe how bright a light is. The National Institute of Standards and Technology measure lumen output using a device called an integration sphere. They use photometers to count light particles inside the sphere.

In 2009, the American National Standards Institute (ANSI) approved a standard for flashlight performance. The resulting specification called ANSI/NEMA FL-1 is designed to help consumers make fair comparisons of lights and to eliminate exaggerated light performance by quoting odd features such as "emitter lumens" or "out-the-front lumens." The manufacturer or an independent lab can perform the tests, however, the necessary equipment and calibration makes this an expensive undertaking. To date, I was only able to find one manufacturer, Light and Motion that tested their lights to this specification and shared the results with consumers. Light and Motion also tested other popular brands and reports comparative results on their website at: www.LightandMotion.com

Duration and Burn Curve

When lumens are tested, the actual runtime should also be reported. Burn time is determined when the light output drops to 10% of its original value using the batteries included with the flashlight. When viewing the test results of competitive light brands on Light and Motion's website it appears that numerous manufacturers are over reporting the intensity and burn time. Some models actually performed at 50% of the claimed specification. None of the lights listed in the comparison charts performed better than their advertised quality when tested to the FL-1 standard! It is also interesting to view the burn curves on the graphs to determine whether a light maintains brightness over the duration or whether it quickly lowers intensity to lengthen burn time. As a videographer, I want a light with a consistently bright beam.

Beam Quality and Coverage

Early underwater video lights utilized wide dimpled metal reflectors to spread the beam of light. Some employed translucent diffusers to improve the dispersion of the beam. Newer, low profile reflector solutions and LED angles can create a soft and even light beam with a wide range of coverage. Look for a light that does not have hot spots and that evenly covers a wide area. A lighting manufacturer usually specifies whether a light is a "spot" or a "flood" and should indicate how many degrees of coverage the device will deliver.

Seek out technical specifications before spending a lot of money on video lights. Light and Motion compares tests for popular lights on the website: LightandMotion.com

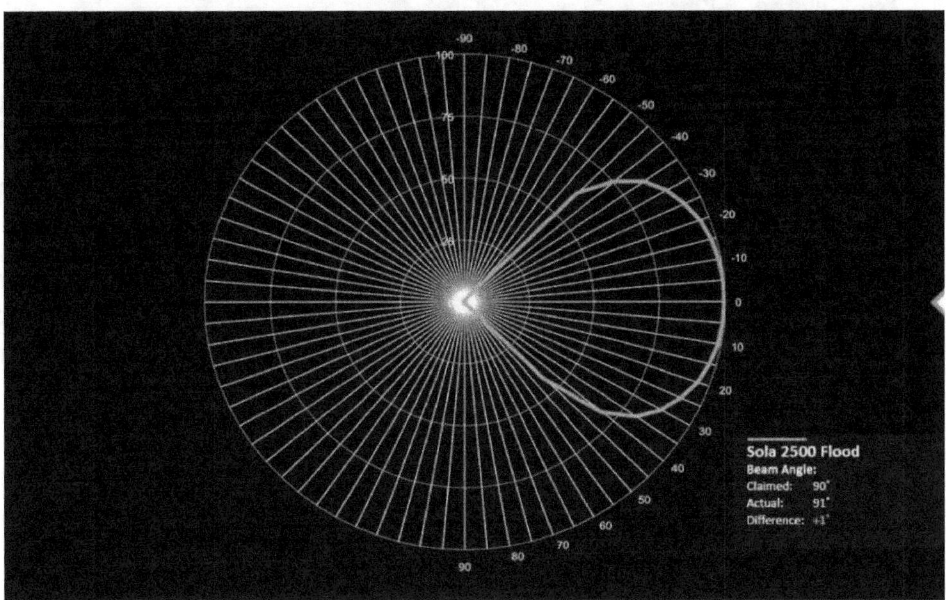

Purpose/Multipurpose

The best video lights are expensive, yes, but they may offer the benefit of multi function capability. Some lights can be dimmed and used as primary lights for technical diving. Some offer focusable lenses that narrow a beam to a more suitable angle of coverage for cave and wreck diving.

Weight, Size and Buoyancy

I have often struggled with American airport security, the TSA, when trying to fly with large battery packs and cinema lights. There is a limit to the size of lithium batteries that are allowed on a commercial aircraft. Smaller, lighter units can be easily flown without challenge from airport security. Buoyancy characteristics are also important. Lights are often affixed to long extension arms. Negatively buoyant light heads can be problematic and tiring to swim for any length of time..

Company Reputation

A video light is an investment and it may need service in the future. Buying lights that are made as close to home as possible from a reputable company makes sense. Customer service, reputation, innovation and warranty are all issues to explore. A company's customer service reputation may be as important as the units they sell. Ask around, and get opinions from other divers.

Environmental Impact

There are many way that a manufacturer can be environmentally responsible. Using recycled materials, rechargeable batteries and a local workforce will all reduce the environmental impact. If the light has rechargeable batteries it may save significant money over the life of the product. Consider the operating cost to your wallet, and the environment, in your purchase decision.

Purchasing quality video lights takes some serious research. But as you are gliding effortlessly over a colorful reef while enjoying the vibrant colors of the underwater world, you will know it was an investment worth making.

Shooting Macro

Up Close and Personal

Shooting a majestic wreck in clear water or a passing whale shark might be the biggest underwater video opportunity of a lifetime. However, there are plenty of magnificent tiny subjects to be found in both freshwater and ocean environments. Shooting close up or macro, as we refer to it, can be addicting. Once you slow down and move in, you may get hooked on filming the tiny inhabitants of the underwater world.

Depending on your camera and housing, you may need some gear modifications to get the best out of macro videography. If you have a dedicated video camera in a housing, you may be able to zoom in to shoot macro. Some housings offer "zoom-through" lenses as a front port. This type of glass will permit you to focus at full zoom on the video camera's lens. Other camera and housing combinations may not permit sharp focus at full zoom. Some housings are further equipped with a flip up or down diopter that magnifies the scene without needing to switch domes or lenses. A Macromate style wet lens can also be added to some housings. This magnifier snaps on the exterior and traps water between the magnifier and the housing. These are available for many cameras and can also be custom manufactured for unique camera housings.

If you are shooting macro with a DSLR and housing, there may be a little more preparation involved. To begin, you will need to switch out your camera lens to something in the range of 50-100mm focal length. Shorter focal length lenses are easiest to begin with. Larger focal lengths will fill the frame with smaller creatures but are trickier to focus due to minimal depth of field. 100mm lenses are also more challenging because you have to shoot from farther away and therefore your light source will need much more "punch" to get the best exposure. When you change your camera lens, you will also have to switch your dome port to a macro port. An extension tube and focus gear may also be required to enable manual focus.

Regardless of the type of camera you are using, you will need some form of stabilization. This will make it easier to focus and control camera shake. You might start with a simple and inexpensive Gorilla pod or move up to a more capable underwater tripod with extendable legs. The best underwater tripods can also pan and tilt. In either case, you should be very careful to avoid damaging the environment. It may be okay to set a tripod in a clear patch of sand, but never on live reef. Lightweight tripods may need to be weighted to stay in place if there is a surge or strong current. Hang the weight from the center of the tripod to minimize your footprint. If your subject is moving, you can use a single leg of the tripod braced against your arm to help stabilize your footage.

Video lights are critical for shooting good macro footage. They enable you to use smaller apertures, and increase depth of field. Ideally you will need two lights. The first light is known as the key, or main light. Illuminate the subject with the main light at a 45° angle. The second light, known as the fill light, can illuminate details and fill the shadows if you point it directly down on the subject. One downside of powerful lights is that you may have a more difficult time capturing natural underwater life behavior.

When you start shooting macro, you should choose stationary or slow moving subjects that can't swim away. You have to exercise patience, and use your excellent buoyancy skills to avoid kicking up silt that will ruin your shot or scare your subject back into its home. At first, you may want to find and select a single subject for a dive. If you calmly wait, you will be rewarded when the marine life returns to its normal behavior, as it believes the risk of your presence has passed.

Shooting charismatic mega-fauna may be an adrenaline filled encounter, but once you capture a rare Frog Fish or colorful nudibranchs entwined in the reef, you will find a whole new interest in identifying and cataloguing the tiny inhabitants of our oceans and lakes.

Shooting Big Animals in Open Ocean

I roll over the edge of the Zodiac with my camera and housing in my lap. There is no other choice. With the ripping current, I have to take everything I need and swim as fast as possible, sprinting for the down line. In the middle of the Atlantic, off the Azorean paradise of Santa Maria Island, I have one brief opportunity to capture the majestic beauty of the endangered Devil Ray. The locals call them "jamanta" and they attract divers to this remote seamount for the chance to have a close encounter in the clear blue water. Despite the visual clarity, the shooting conditions could not be tougher. When you are shooting large animals in open water you are filming unpredictable creatures with no control over their direction, and if you are me on this day, they are swimming directly at me, backlit by the blazing sun, with 12 stops of contrast and sunlight illuminating every bubble that drifts in front of my lens. When the opportunity to shoot big marine animals is short, it pays to be organized from the moment you hit the water.

- Get your gear ready and checked early so nothing delays you from being first off the boat. Beware of over heating on deck, and douse your head with water if it gets uncomfortable.
- Preset your camera controls such as exposure, white balance and ISO and test shoot a short sequence to ensure everything is right before hitting the water.
- Make sure your card has been reformatted so you have lots of room for footage.
- Pre-focus on something topside, at the approximate distance that you anticipate between you and your animal subject, and hit record before you roll off the boat. Sometimes your only animal interaction will happen in the first few seconds you are in the water. Don't miss it! (Besides, you might actually use the roll shot in your final edit!)
- Point your dome toward your belly when you roll and make sure nothing will hit the camera or scratch the dome port.
- Once safely in the water, wipe the fine bubbles off the lens and point the camera towards the action.

- If you see a smudge on the dome, lick it off with your tongue! It's just like defogging a mask.
- Hopefully the boat has a tag line that you can grab to get you to the descent line. Ask for one if they don't. Hold your camera in one hand and pull with the other and pace yourself so you don't get tired before the action even starts.
- Some big animal dives, like the Devil Rays in Santa Maria, are conducted on a descent line. That means that everyone in the group is stacked vertically on a mooring line. Try to take the lowest position on the line to get out of everyone else's bubble stream.
- Free swimmers can easily get swept away from the area or get exhausted in the raging current, so take a john-line to connect you to the vertical mooring line. A john-line consists of a strap or line that is hooked to the descent line and also to the crotch D-ring on a diver's harness for BCD. This permits the diver to be "clipped-in" and work hands free. Inexperienced divers should not clip themselves to anything fixed underwater. In this case, a john-line can also be used as a handgrip.
- In order to stretch beyond the other diver's bubble streams, use a john-line that is longer than anyone else's in the group.
- Minimize accessories on your camera housing in order to make it easy to handle in the current. Lights and strobes may do more to antagonize or scare away the marine life. You might be better off shooting in the ambient light.
- If you stop recording, pre-focus on somebody on the ascent line before pointing your camera into the blue. (You might not be able to grab an auto focus in the low contrast of open water.)
- Shoot upwards for contrast or for silhouetting an animal against the light.
- Move very slowly and hold the camera as still as possible. The dance of the Devil Rays is the appeal of the shot. Fast and erratic movements will ruin your efforts.
- Be careful about over exposure and clipping in the highlight regions. If your camera has "zebras," (a striped shading that shows where the brightest areas of your exposure are located) turn them on and monitor closely.

- Watch your decompression status and air supply. When you are wrapped up in the moment, you might forget to keep track of your life support!
- Empower your dive partner to be extra vigilant and watch over you and your resources.

Having a close encounter with these gentle, graceful giants might be a once in a lifetime opportunity. Be prepared. Pre-visualize your dive. Pre-set as much photo gear as you can. The best part is that, because you were in the right place, totally ready, your remarkable experience is yours to share for a lifetime!

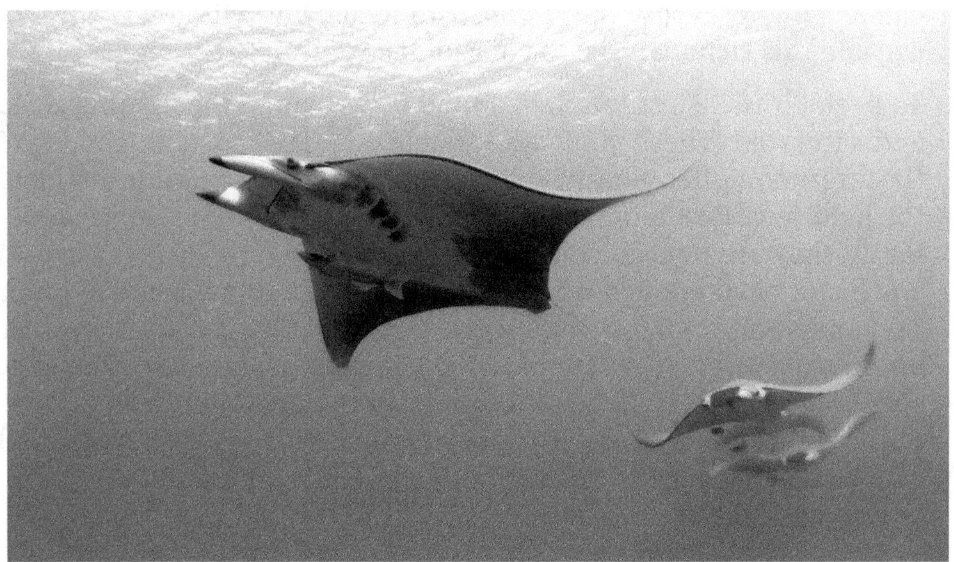

Shooting Devil Fish in the Azores. Photo: Jill Heinerth

Over Under Shooting

Splitting the Difference

We've all seen them: over-under split images that show a dive boat on the surface and a happy diver or colorful marine creature below the surface. These all-in-one images often grace the front covers of dive magazines and featured resort ads. They are compelling shots that provide an additional context and frame of reference to our underwater world. Though we often see these types of images in print publications they are not as common in video content. They can be challenging to expose and difficult to focus, but with a few tips, you can add this rich material to your underwater production.

To begin, it is easiest to select a time of day when the lighting is rich and saturated. These golden hours early in the morning and late in the afternoon offer vibrant colors. The low position of the sun bends the light rays, providing the most vivid natural palettes. More importantly, they are not too contrasty and are therefore easier to expose. You'll still need enough of an angle on the sun to get some illumination underwater, so pick a time and direction that is as close to a balanced exposure above and below the surface as possible. The exposure value topside will be different from the one underwater. This is one case where an auto exposure feature will fall short. Manually expose for the topside subjects and add artificial illumination to the underwater scene.

If you don't quite get the optimum exposure, it is possible to make some corrections in post-production. Use a filter on the upper half of the image to darken it or add a colorcast that gives an illusion of sunset. The resulting sequence can be an intense golden setting, contrasted by the cool aquamarine world below.

Light refraction can pose some issues for an over-under image. You may find that one half of your image is well focused and the other is fuzzy. To increase depth of field, use a wide dome with a fisheye lens to bring everything into sharp focus. The curvature of the dome will distort images at the interface between the over and under point, so play with the angle of the housing to capture either a sharp horizontal interface, or tilt the housing to create a uniquely curved scene juxtaposition. If you plan to hold a long shot at the surface, you will discover that your housing is suddenly very heavy. You may not be able to hold it half out of the water for very long without sinking below the waves. I've used buoyancy wings or Styrofoam boards to support a heavy camera for shots that need to be relatively stable.

When you pop your dome out of the water, you'll find that little rivulets of water will stream down the dome. This can be distracting, especially if the water creates a big blob in the wrong part of your scene. Those water droplets will destroy focus. If you have a glass dome on your camera, a product such as RainX can be applied to the dome to help it shed water. This product may not be safe for your acrylic dome, so check your instruction manual first. Sometimes, evenly licking the lens before the shot will also do the trick.

If you have any scratches in your dome port, this may be the time they rear their ugly head. A scratched dome may fill with water beneath the surface and hide the damage, but topside it will refract light and create an unsightly flare.

I've used lengthy over-under sequences to illustrate the life above and below a river, but more often, I use the over-under to start or end a sequence. At the beginning of a dive, slip into the water without your camera. Have the Divemaster pass it to you, but keep the lens half out of the water to avoid spots and rivulets. Shoot your partner entering the water with a giant stride with the camera lens split and then as they hit the water, tilt down to reveal the glorious swish of water and air mixing as they splash down. This shot will add power and context to the beginning of a dive sequence and elevate your professional quality. As you tilt or pan down, be aware that you may need to compensate for exposure changes. If your camera is set for auto exposure, it may do that for you, but some cameras are better than others. A good camera will smoothly transition to the new exposure, where other cameras may ratchet or jump through stepped exposures. Test your particular equipment out in advance of shooting important scenes to see how it performs.

Of course, this technique can be just as beautiful at the end of a dive. Coach your partner to surface and let out a big smile to close the end of a great video sequence. Look at the available light to ensure their face is illuminated, (rather than backlit,) and plan the shot with them prior to your dive.

Small cameras such as GoPros have the added benefit of being able to enter the water with the camera in hand, and fully transition from above to below. Turn the lens toward your face and hold the camera in your outstretched arm as you roll or giant stride into the water. It goes without saying that this is one case when you want to use a lanyard, just in case you drop the camera during the entry. Safety always needs to come first, but it is good to know you won't lose your investment if you need to catch a mask or grab your regulator.

Invest the time to practice and experiment with over-under shots and you'll be pleased with the ultimate dynamic video dividends.

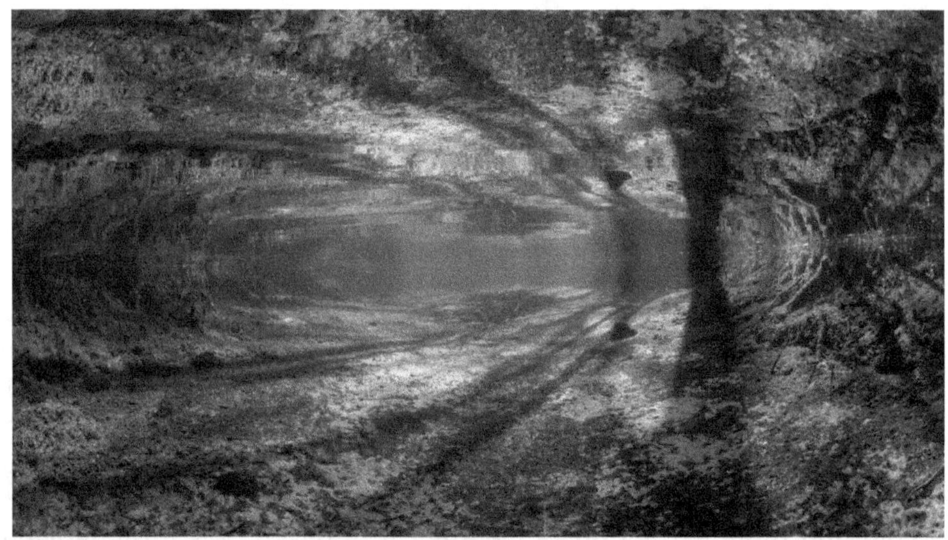

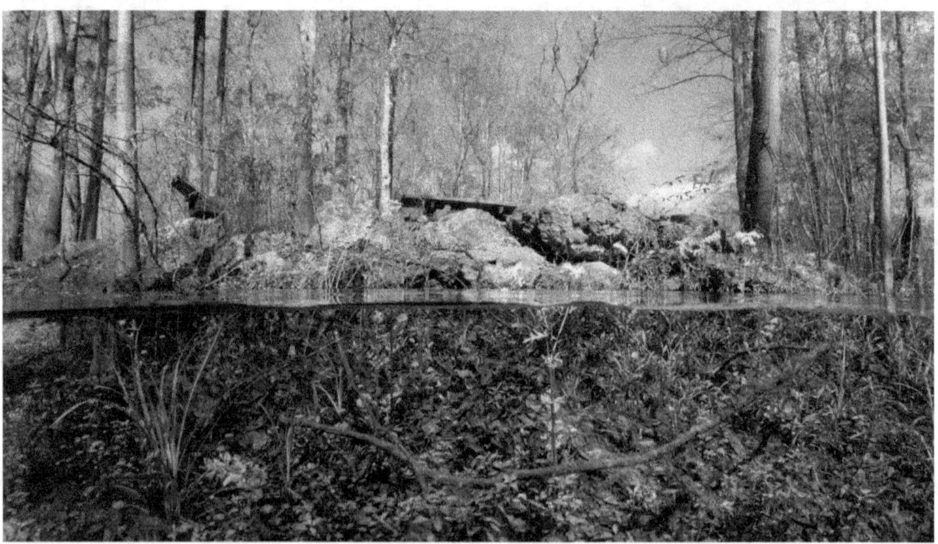

Footage shot near or at the surface is interesting. In the right lighting conditions, you can capture a perfectly mirrored reflection. Photos: Jill Heinerth

Protecting Your Investment

It was not easy climbing down to the cave entrance with hundreds of pounds of video and lighting equipment. Every step was a careful dance, cradling the HD camera and Amphibico housing that was worth more than my car. We had scratched a dome port in transport the day before. It was the third port we had damaged on this one-month National Geographic shoot in central Mexico. Every time we ground the lens against the wall of the cave or allowed it to get battered in transport, the cash register rang up another $1800. Cinematographer Wes Skiles seemed somewhat ambivalent, "you can't worry too much about damaging the gear. It is the cost of getting footage nobody has seen before."

On this dive, I descended into the murky depths of Cenote Ucil with Joel Tower shooting while Wes was carefully monitoring the feed from above. Joel zeroed in on the details of my rebreather, filming cutaways and close-ups as a small ROV dropped down beside me. It steered into position and I reached out with my finger extended, mimicking Michelangelo's Sistine Chapel masterpiece, touching the God-like techno creature that was to continue to explore beyond my human limits. I turned to face the camera to repeat the shot, offering Joel a chance to film the ROV's point of view. I stared into the dome and reached out towards the camera port. It was a beautiful moment until I realized that there was a pool of water sloshing around on the inside of the housing. I can only imagine Wes's shock as I reacted to the flood, gesticulating wildly straight into the camera. Go up! Go up! It was the last I saw of Joel until after my deco. He rocketed upwards, passing off the camera to safety divers who would carry the precious cargo to the topside crew. We all felt a lump in our throats. This looked a little more expensive than $1800.

Unless you are a professional underwater videographer it is doubtful that you'll ever have to make that level of continual investment in your video system. These days, many video packages are reasonably inexpensive and remarkably capable. Some of the footage shot today on consumer cameras could closely rival the quality we were able to shoot on a quarter-million dollar Sony system fifteen years ago. Regardless, your camera is a hard-earned investment, so protecting it properly is important. There are a few things you can do to lessen the likelihood of having a flood and some key maintenance efforts you can make if you have a bad day out.

Fixing Scratches

If you invested in a glass dome port it is far less likely to get scratched than an acrylic dome. Unfortunately there is really no remedy for a scratch on a glass dome. If the gouge is shallow, the water will likely "fill in" the mark unless you point the camera upward and catch the sunlight at a bad angle. If you own an acrylic dome, it can be repaired with a little investment in time and patience.

Before choosing to repair a scratch, be sure you need to! It takes time and you should only sand down a dome two or three times at most before replacing it completely. Begin by purchasing a micro-mesh dome port repair kit. If possible, remove the hood from the dome so you can fully access the front surface. Even though the scratch is small, you must uniformly wet sand the entire acrylic face. Using a series of up to ten different sand papers, you will rough up the entire dome in straight uniform passes. Each stage is going to take about 15 minutes. When you start the process the first time, you will be horrified at the thought of destroying the entire surface. You will have moments when you question whether this is a good idea at all. But, as you slowly work towards finer and finer papers, it will be restored "as smooth as glass." Take your time and carefully follow instructions in the kit. Dry and save each piece of sandpaper so you can reuse them if you scratch the dome again.

It is rare, but sometimes people scratch the inside of the port when they accidentally drop a camera component inside the housing. In this case, it is much more difficult to effectively sand the inside surface. You could end up with some non-uniform spots around the edge of the dome, but fortunately, they usually fall outside of the field of view.

With a little care and prevention you may never have to experience the trauma of a scratch or a flood. But remember, it's only photo gear. Never compromise your safety because of a piece of damaged gear. Your safety is the most important thing. Equipment can easily be repaired or replaced.

Insurance

Consider purchasing specialized insurance for your underwater imaging equipment. Some homeowner policies will allow you to place a special rider on your contract but a claim may come with high deductibles and future penalties. Divers Alert Network sponsors insurance for equipment through a third-party insurer. I have used this insurance and found it to be hassle-free. The coverage includes floods and offers full replacement value based on your stated value. There is a deductible for flooding, but if the gear is stolen or lost in airline transport, they will cover the entire stated value. These days you have almost no choice but to put your expensive system in checked baggage, so it is good to know that DAN sponsored insurance will help you out if the TSA kicks it across the terminal.

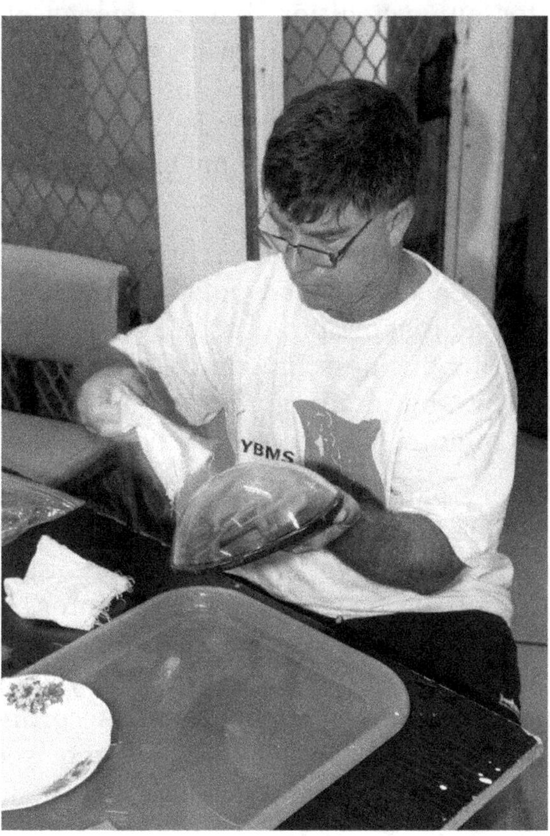

Brian Kakuk works on carefully polishing a scratched dome port while in the field in Christmas Island. Photo: Jill Heinerth

Digital Workflow

Project Planning

What's Your Story?

While filling our flimsy paper plates with a sampling of cold cuts and cheese, Wes Skiles and I brainstormed about our upcoming trip to Antarctica. The largest iceberg in recorded history had calved off the Ross Ice Shelf and we were going to intercept it. National Geographic had approved the funding for our expedition, but the money was limited and so was the crew. Wes looked up from his potato salad, "Jill, you need to do double duty on this project. I want you organize our diving, but more importantly, you need to write and produce our film." With spicy brown mustard dribbling down my chin, I replied, "sure thing Wes. What's a producer?"

Wes and I had been working together on television projects, always pushing the bounds of my experience, but this would be a big leap. I had helped him write copy and edit short projects, but never a full-length documentary. My previous business in Canada had involved advertising and commercial work, but crafting a message of 30 seconds was far different than 90 minutes. Where would I begin?

Luckily, I had the help of a very patient industry giant Bill Kurtis, whose daily encouragement guided me through the journey of storytelling. He would co-produce the film, helping us to gain additional funding and distribution. Additionally, he would act as a mentor and editor for my work. "What's the story?" he asked me during our first phone call. The industry nomenclature is "log line." How do you describe your story in a single sentence or short paragraph? According to Kurtis, if you can't describe your story in a single phrase or sentence, then you better not even start writing the script.

Consider a typical slasher movie. The log lines are all the same. "It's a story about a bunch of college kids that go away for a weekend and get cut up by a demon with a chainsaw." Most diving films never reach this level of story development. Most diving films are simply travelogs. They are simply a chronicle of a series of dives in a new place. A great diving film needs a log line to give it direction. Envision these two alternatives. If your family goes on a vacation to Crystal River, you could shoot travel log of the trip, but if you want to be creative you could shoot a story with a log line. "Its a story about a young girl's first encounter with an injured manatee that changes her direction in life to pursue veterinary medicine." For tropical divers it might be something like, "its the story about a Bonaire native, whose opportunity to dive elevates him to create the island's first eco resort" or "it's a story about a diver's quest to discover an elusive sea horse in the tangled ecosystem of a Bahamian reef."

I settled with the log line, "It's a story about an international crew that follows the path of the legendary Ernest Shackleton a century after his ill fated journey through the virgin wilderness of the Antarctic ice pack, while experiencing first hand a rapidly changing climate and effects of global warming." It was weak and way too complicated, but Bill Kurtis urged me to begin writing the script. I spent months immersing myself in Shackleton's story and his legendary leadership, realizing that we might encounter some of the serious challenges he faced. His journey left him locked in the ice. Our trip would be about the breakup of that same ice shelf. Climate change was a new and politically charged term, but I read everything I could find on the subject. I spent months carefully crafting my words and sketching a vision with storyboards. But despite my best-laid plans, I was still a neophyte, with much to learn about expedition filmmaking.

Some thirty days into our project we were parked beside a great mass of grounded ice, which had lodged itself on the sea floor at Cape Hallett. We had faced great difficulties before arriving at this place, but with our trip only half-completed, we were running low on fuel. We needed to spend some time here in the bergs and pack ice to try to capture our story. I wasn't feeling the parallel to Shackleton. We had been stuck in the ice for a couple of days, but I felt protected in this safe harbor. The trip was tough, but it had no relation to a two-year epic of survival on the ice and in a lifeboat. I felt our story floundering. If I could have talked to Bill Kurtis at that moment he would have certainly offered some guidance, but there was no connection to the outside world, no phone calls, emails or contact with society. I hadn't even seen a contrail in the sky for a month. In the freshness of a heavy twilight blizzard Wes and I stood on deck catching giant snowflakes on our faces. He said, "just be prepared to shift gears when a new story emerges. Don't lose sight of the experience you are having because the story you expected is not happening." I understood immediately. Sometimes you need a slap in the face to see the real story before you.

In the cold light of the following morning, Paul Heinerth and I completed the first-ever cave dive inside an iceberg cave. Over the course of the next weeks we experienced a calving that blocked the entrance to our cave, we were sucked through a berg by raging currents and discovered and ecosystem that had never been documented. But the real story came to me about an hour after we took Wes on a filming dive inside our new cave. Over a meal of canned spaghetti on toast with a side of slightly moldy pumpkin, our iceberg cave suddenly heaved and hollered, summoning us up to the deck of the ship. With a full moon current ripping at the fabric of the ice, it shattered before us, heaving a wall of water into the evening sky. Our cave was destroyed itself in a matter of minutes. Mother Nature was urging us to head home. Our journey inside the ice was done.

Ice Island: In spring of 2000, the largest moving object ever seen on our planet began its voyage - so grand in scale it changed the earth's rotation as it moved. A special team from the National Geographic Society and the New England Aquarium are the first to employ a bold new technological approach at exploring above, below and within the ice. But despite the natural beauty that captivates them, they are in a race to escape the clutches of the ice. How will they get out?

As divers, we often experience the uncommon and the unexpected. The next time you have an opportunity to shoot, think about a log line that will direct your story, but always be prepared to shift gears and tell the surprising tale that reveals itself on your remarkable journey into our water planet.

Shooting

The second step in digital workflow is acquisition of material. We've covered this, so we'll keep moving.

Downloading

The third step in the digital workflow process happens after the dive and involves downloading the images from the camera for storage on a computer or one or more hard disks or DVDs.

There are two ways to download images from your camera to your computer. Each technique has its inherent advantages and disadvantages.

• USB Connection

Some prefers connecting the camera to the computer via USB port since there is little risk of damaging the memory card since it is never taken out of the camera. The card slot is also kept very clean since it is rarely opened. The disadvantage is that a voltage spike through your computer may damage the computer, the camera and the images on the card. When traveling in locations with unreliable power, it is worth keeping this in mind. Similarly, a sudden loss of camera battery power could result in lost or corrupted data.

• Using Card Readers

Once you have removed the memory card from your camera, it can be inserted into a card reader that hooks up to the USB port on your computer. In this case a power spike could damage the computer and card reader, but not the camera. The drawback of card readers is that their inexpensive technology sometimes fails and this could result in loss of data. However, if you shoot a lot, you can download from multiple readers simultaneously. The newest cameras offer wireless transfer of images to your computer or the Internet.

Many cameras come with proprietary software that launches automatically as soon as you plug in the USB port. It is not necessary to use these programs. Your memory card is just like a hard drive. It will appear on your desktop and you can simply drag the files from the card to either your computer or an external hard drive. You can change Preferences in software so they don't launch automatically.

You can simultaneously drag and drop the photos to a computer and an external hard drive so that you have an immediate backup of your files. Many people also make DVD back-ups, but if you do so, you should recopy those DVDs every couple of years or so. Do not consider DVDs to be permanent, archival storage.

Once the images are downloaded from the memory card, it is preferable to reformat the card rather than simply deleting the files. When you delete a file, there are remnants left on a card since you have only truly deleted the index and not all the data. The remaining artifacts also take up critical space on the card. It is advisable to reformat to maximize available space and lessen the chance of file corruption down the road.

Organizing, Sorting and Ingesting Your Files

The fourth step in the digital workflow process involves organizing your files with metadata. Many programs like Final CutX or Adobe Premiere allow you to add keywords to the file by either typing in words or checking boxes of commonly used keywords like "cave" or "shark." You can get as detailed as you wish with keywords, but critical information like location, model's name, etc. should always be noted so that you may search for an sequence with those keywords later.

You can discard poor shots and accidental rolls at this point because your next step is to Import or Ingest the media into the computer. This step creates a low-res Proxy file that you can quickly work with and links it to the original material in a way that can assemble the final program after your edit.

Editing the Program

There are numerous editing programs available from Final CutX to Premiere to CineForm and QuickTime Pro. Some editing programs are available as free or inexpensive apps, while others are sold as subscription services with a monthly fee. An entire book can be written about editing and is beyond the reach of this edition. Use online forums, YouTube tutorials and teaching platforms such as Udemy or LFE.com to find good introductory classes in editing.

Audio

Voice Over

As you edit you may want to add an audio voice over track. This can be done through your computer mic, but it is far better to narrate with a better microphone. Audio is often given short shrift. It deserves attention to quality. Here are a few key tips:

1. Consider background noise in the room in which you are recording. Is there a fan running and creating white noise? Is the fridge making a distracting hum? (Note: If you turn off the fridge, put you car keys in the freezer. It makes it more likely that you won't ruin an entire fridge of food, because you'll need those keys sooner than later and will be reminded about turning it back on!)
2. Buy a decent microphone. The Blue Icicle is a great model and Rode makes numerous good quality mics. If you can't afford those, try a headphone-mounted mic, but check to make sure it does not sound too stifled.
3. Listen for the letters "s" and "p." Do they hiss or pop? This can be annoying. A pop filter will help or reposition the mic to reduce the annoying sounds.
4. Record audio between -6 and -12dB. Low audio levels are tough to recover without bringing up background noise too.
5. Write a script to guide your message, but try to act natural and speak as though you are telling a friend about your message.

Natural Sound

The "nat" sound track is important to the story too. Even with a voice over track, it is good to hear the steady rhythm of the bubbles from the original track. Check levels so they are not overwhelming the voice or music tracks.

How to Use Music in Your Videos without Breaking the Law

As you drift into the alluring darkness of Highbourne Wall in the Exuma Islands, you spot a graceful eagle ray swimming up from the abyss. The ear worm of Tom Petty's song "Free Fallin'" is drilling into your head. You know that will be the perfect music to accompany your underwater footage. You already have the .mp3 file in your computer, so it should be simple to drop the file into the timeline of your video masterpiece.

Not so fast... Simply said, easy Internet access has changed people's perception of creative media ownership. People who would never consider shoplifting, seem to feel comfortable stealing and redistributing intellectual property such as photographs, music and videos. However, you might be completely unaware of your own participation in copyright infringement until you receive a legal notice from YouTube. Although your video may only attract a few hundred views by friends and family, a sophisticated software robot has discovered your indiscretion – innocently using your favorite Tom Petty tune on your vacation video. This column will help you safely navigate the muddy waters of licensing music for your video products. Copyright law is complicated, so clearly, I cannot offer legal advice, but I can offer some guidance to help you avoid the most common mistakes of amateur videographers.

If you want to guarantee to avoid copyright violations, then you need to create completely original content. Although programs such as Garage Band make this possible, few people take this path. Finding and licensing music is therefore one of the only viable options. Even songs as ubiquitous as the "Happy Birthday" song require licensing. The owners of that little ditty, (Warner-Chappell publishing) are well known as rabid defenders of their property. Even singing it on video can attract a lawyer.

In a nutshell, you may use works that are in the "public domain." Most pieces recorded prior to 1922 are in the public domain in the U.S., but specific recordings are not. In other words, a song may not require licensing, but the performers or producers may need to be compensated if you use a specific recording.

"Royalty Free" music may be free to use, but it does not necessarily live in the public domain. Permission must be granted for use. In many cases, the permission is a blanket permission that is very easy to obtain. In other cases, such as with the popular American musician Moby, he grants royalty free use of certain of his recordings by not-for-profit projects that reflect his passion for specific environmental and social causes. In still other cases, there may be a small fee for the music license itself. You can search online using the terms "royalty free music" or go to popular sources including:

Kevin MacLeod's www.incompetech.com or www.youtube.com/audiolibrary/music.

Professional music libraries are a great option for variety and quality. Technical diving instructor Randy Thornton, Chairman of Amphibious Zoo Music, says, "when choosing which music to use for your project, keep in mind that securing music rights can be a somewhat complicated and expensive process if you are trying to secure rights from a record label or music publisher. Typically, you would need rights for both the recorded material as well as the music publisher rights, all of which might be controlled by multiple parties. An easier approach is to license music from a production music library, which typically contains all necessary rights bundled in one transaction. Additionally, production music libraries price their content to fit the user's budget."

These music libraries allow you to purchase a single track, an album of tracks or even an entire library of music with specific usage agreements. Typically songs will be broken down into shorter segments as well. Oftentimes, you may purchase a theme, a variation(s), short "stingers" and related content in 30 and 60 second bites. This family of music will help in the editing process and give you a truly finished and professional piece. Depending on your use and exclusivity requirements, you could pay anything from a dollar to thousands.

Penalties for stealing music can be significant, especially is you are monetizing your video. Beyond legal actions, other things can happen. YouTube may suspend your upload privileges. They may mute your audio or they may place ads on your content with benefits supporting YouTube and the original artist(s) and publisher. Their sophisticated tracking system "ContentID" is constantly scanning new uploads. They flag thousands of videos every day and may require you to produce your license or face action.

It's okay to listen to your favorite tunes on your underwater .mp3 player, but when it comes time to edit your video, be very careful about selecting music that you may legally use. Get the correct permissions and clearances, save the paperwork, and you can rest assured you'll stay out of trouble with creative content providers and publishers.

Saving the Sequence

After the sequence has been edited, it is important to save it in an appropriate format. Depending on whether you are planning on showing your piece at a Film Festival or on Vimeo or a cell phone, you will choose a different format. There is no sense saving a huge file for Internet consumption, when your viewers don't have bandwidth to watch it. Similarly, if a file is too large for a computer/projector combination, it might choke and stutter on screen. Many Save and Export options are available in editing programs. If the correct setting is not available, then a program such as Compressor will help you save in an appropriate manner.

Choosing the Best Free Video Sharing Services

Every single minute, more than 72 hours of new video content is uploaded to YouTube. In an average month, people around the world watch 4 billion hours on the YouTube platform, and it has grown to become the second largest search engine on the planet. YouTube is now as ubiquitous as the likelihood of seeing cat videos in your inbox! But there are other options available for sharing your underwater videos and each has specific benefits and drawbacks.

YouTube

Since it is owned by Google, using YouTube may increase your chances of showing up in online searches. As a free service, it is hard to imagine that it still permits unlimited uploads. If you are trying to create a platform, you can build your own "channel" with customizable backgrounds and personal playlists. Businesses may also take advantage of advertising plans that will enhance visibility. Being able to distribute your content in many resolutions is also a huge asset. Viewers with fast connections can enjoy the highest resolution, yet individuals with poor Internet speeds can still see your work in lower resolution. YouTube is the most popular video-sharing platform. Viewers with Twitter re-tweeted YouTube references 50:1 over videos referencing works on Vimeo. The dark side of YouTube is the background noise. Any search may net a frustrating and cluttered collection of poor quality videos and dubious content. It is easy to get lost in the YouTube din. Almost all videos have some type of advertising in the form of an opening clip or lower third content bar. These can obstruct the view of your video. Even if your film is short, it may open with a 30-second commercial that causes your viewers to lose interest.

Vimeo

Vimeo is often the preferred platform for creative professionals. The interface is more streamlined and aesthetically appealing and can be organized as a private channel that shuts out the competing video content of other providers. Vimeo permits longer films, a larger viewing window and filters out commercial videos, advertisements and other content that is not produced by the user owning the account. The feature I like best is the ability to select the thumbnail that represents your video. You can scan through your content and select the frame that really tells the story. You can also set privacy settings that allow you to maintain complete privacy or share with a select group through a password. This can be as important for development content as it might be for family videos. If you want to raise your profile to professional status, you can add your own logo and format the channel page so that is blends beautifully with your corporate image. You can also create feedback forums that currently seem less susceptible to hacker commenting and hijacking by bots that are trying to commandeer the search engine results you have worked hard to create. Although Vimeo's viewing audience is smaller, it may bring more serious viewers to your page. They don't have to wade as deeply through the piano-playing kitty's to find your work, as they might on YouTube. The biggest drawback for Vimeo is that the upload speed is throttled down for free users. To get a faster upload and unlimited HD uploads, you'll have to move up to the premium accounts for a fee. Additionally, your video may not enjoy the same level of Google search engine optimization that it would on YouTube.

Vine

If you captured an amazing moment of a humpback whale breaching or rare coral spawning, then this platform may be perfect to showcase your short segment. Vine is growing quickly into a viable option for sharing short content videos on mobile devices. Vine's popularity may be partly due to the open dialogue between users and viewers. Their limitation in clip length also seems to power creativity. If your browse through Vine you are likely to come across some very interesting things. Be advised that Vine does not have any filters against adult content. Your professional work will be commingled with potentially offensive clips that may not be suitable for all viewers.

Instagram

Instagram has reached a younger demographic in a way other platforms have failed. If you build a credible profile you can use this as effective marketing for your personal brand. By choosing to use Instagram as a community platform, you can interact with other users who can help elevate your profile. Instagram links well with other social media platforms like Twitter. If you use hash tags (#) in your content, you will help people to find your work. Facebook currently owns Instagram and that means the two work very well together. Users are provided with up to 15 seconds of a single video and you can edit this clip and the thumbnail in the platform itself. The biggest disadvantage beyond the short length of content is that the Instagram file is not embeddable and cannot be looped as it can with Vine.

File Sizes

Many video cameras generate enormous files in 4K and larger. This may be more than your Internet service can easily manage. Large files may require significant bandwidth to upload and post and if you live in a rural part of North America, your bandwidth may be limited or throttled. Keep the files as small as possible so you don't consume your Wifi allowance or overwhelm your friend's browser. People will generally accept lower resolution better than a video that chokes when they try to view it, so consider optimizing the file size and use a lower resolution than you originally captured.

Whether you are an amateur videographer sharing content with friends or a budding professional trying to build an Internet brand, you'll eventually upload your work for others to see. Remember to put a credit on your video short so that when other people embed your work, it can still be tracked back to you as the creator. You never know when your short of the leaping Great White Shark might go viral. Then again, keep making videos of your cute cat's antics. That's a sure thing.

Conclusions

It's tough to encapsulate the experience of shooting in a way that covers an audience that includes both GoPro users and semi-professional filmmakers. The one piece of advice that I can offer to everyone is one of general encouragement. We live in an interesting time. The old gatekeepers that used to control TV have no relevancy any more. If you want to be a filmmaker, then you can be one. Nobody has to give you permission. You can start your own website and open a YouTube Channel and you are in business. Of course, you will still need to drive the viewers to your door, but the only thing stopping you is practice and courage. Shoot lots, post lots and participate in the dialogue online and you can build your personal brand. Reach out to commissioning producers with your material. Propose well-imagined projects for expeditions to funding entities or simply share with your family and friends. Underwater cameras have inspired a generation to participate in diving. Hopefully the new explosion of material will help us forge a better future for our underwater world.

More Products by Heinerth Productions Inc.

Books

The Basics of Rebreather Diving

Women Underwater

The Essentials of Cave Diving

Chester the Manatee and the Very, Very, Terribly Bad Itch (available in numerous languages)

Sidemount Profiles

Movies

We Are Water
Sidemount Diving
Real Sobriety

All books and movies are available on Amazon.com and www.IntoThePlanet.com/buy

www.ingramcontent.com/pod-product-compliance
Lightning Source LLC
LaVergne TN
LVHW080311110826
845155LV00023B/111

* 9 7 8 1 9 4 0 9 4 4 2 1 0 *